Reading for the Citizen of the World
世界公民读本（文库）

R G Reading for the Citizen of the World
世界公民读本〔文库〕

Foundations of Democracy

# 民主的基础丛书

主编 赵文彤

# Responsibility

# 责任

〔美〕Center for Civic Education (公民教育中心) 著

赵文彤 译

隐私
**PRIVACY**

责任
**RESPONSIBILITY**

正义
**JUSTICE**

权威
**AUTHORITY**

金城出版社
GOLD WALL PRESS

FOUNDATIONS of DEMOCRACY

AUTHORITY PRIVACY RESPONSIBILITY JUSTICE

English Edition Copyright ©2009. Center for Civic Education. Calabasas, CA, USA.

著作权合同登记图字：B11002793-01-2011-3498


图书在版编目(CIP)数据

责任 /（美国）公民教育中心著；赵文彤译
—北京：金城出版社，2011.6
（世界公民读本文库/赵文彤主编）
书名原文：Responsibility
ISBN 978-7-80251-926-8

Ⅰ．①责… Ⅱ．①美… ②赵… Ⅲ．①责任感
-青年读物②责任感-少年读物 Ⅳ．①B822.9-49

中国版本图书馆CIP数据核字（2011）第075250号


**责任**

| | |
|---|---|
| 作　　者 | CENTER FOR CIVIC EDUCATION(美国)公民教育中心 |
| 责任编辑 | 袁东旭 |
| 开　　本 | 710毫米×1000毫米 1/16 |
| 印　　张 | 13.75 |
| 字　　数 | 218千字 |
| 版　　次 | 2011年8月第1版 2011年8月第1次印刷 |
| 印　　刷 | 北京联兴华印刷厂 |
| 书　　号 | ISBN 978-7-80251-926-8 |
| 定　　价 | 30.00元 |

| | |
|---|---|
| 出版发行 | **金城出版社** 北京市朝阳区和平街11区37号楼 邮编：100013 |
| 发 行 部 | (010)84254364 |
| 编 辑 部 | (010)64210080 |
| 总 编 室 | (010)64228516 |
| 网　　址 | http://www.jccb.com.cn |
| 电子邮箱 | jinchengchuban@163.com |
| 法律顾问 | 陈鹰律师事务所 （010)64970501 |

## 本书承蒙郭昌明基金资助印行

该基金以一位年近百岁的母亲的名字命名，她和中国近百年来一代又一代的普通母亲一样，将自己对人生和世界最美好的希望全部寄托给了成长中的中国式的世界公民。

The mission of the Center for Civic Education is to promote an enlightened, competent, and responsible citizenry. The curriculum materials prepared under this mandate are designed to advance this outcome. It is our goal to share these materials as widely as possible, to make them available to the students, teachers, and parents of the world, and not to limit distribution or to make profits for any individual.

美国公民教育中心以提高全体公民的文明程度、能力素养和责任感为己任，据此编写的课程教材，为达到这一结果而设计。我们的目标是尽可能广泛地分享这些课程教材，让世界上的学生、教师和家长都可以受用，不受限制地分发，也不为任何个人谋取利益。

**CENTER FOR CIVIC EDUCATION**

5145 Douglas Fir Road

Calabasas, CA 91302 - USA

818.591.9321 - Fax 818.591.9330

cce@civiced.org

www.civiced.org

# 人类命运与责任共同体时代呼唤世界公民

## ——世界公民读本（文库）出版说明

刘建华

## 引子

早在大约 250 年前，中国与世界公民（The Citizen of the World）这个英文词组，就有过一次美丽的的邂逅。18 世纪 60 年代，中国在西方的许多思想家那里，被理想化为一个美好而神秘的国度，哥德斯密（Oliver Goldsmith，1728—1774）就是在这样的时代背景下，以"中国人的信札"（Chinese Letters）为名，发表连载文章，借此讥讽英国的社会弊病，两年后（1763）结集出版，题名为：The Citizen of the World or Letters of a Chinese Philosopher living in London to his Friends in the East. 翻译成中文，是《世界公民—— 一位旅居伦敦的中国哲学家写给他的东方朋友的信札》。

此后过了约 150 年，大约距今 100 年前的 1914 年，一个在美国的中国人应验了歌德斯密的这个噱头式的玩笑。根据邵建先生发表在《大学人文》（广西师范大学出版社 2008 年 5 月版）的文章，这一年，在美国康奈尔大学的学生宿舍里，胡适在自己的一篇日记中，以《大同主义之先哲名言》为题，抄录了以下数则关于"世界公民"的先哲名言，这些名言以无言的方式，影响了无数个"胡适"们，并通过他们在后来的一个世纪里影响了无数中国人——

亚里斯提卜说过，智者的祖国就是世界。
——第欧根尼·拉尔修：《亚里斯提卜》第十三章

当有人问及他是何国之人时，第欧根尼回答道：

"我是世界之公民。"

——第欧根尼·拉尔修：《亚里斯提卜》第十三章

苏格拉底说，他既不是一个雅典人，也不是一个希腊人，

只不过是一个世界公民。

——普卢塔：《流放论》

我的祖国是世界，我的宗教是行善。

——T. 潘恩：《人类的权利》第五章

世界是我的祖国，人类是我的同胞。

——W.L. 加里森：《解放者简介》

一

　　进入 21 世纪以来，全球气候变暖的危机日益明显，与此相关的多种全球性危机日益增多，人类仿佛在一夜之间变得比以往任何时代都更加亲如兄弟、情同手足，地球比以往任何时候都更像是一个风雨飘摇中的小小的村落。这不只是全球经济一体化和信息技术与交通高度发达的结果，也不只是人类追求世界大同理想社会的结果，而是任何一个国家和民族都无法单独应对的全球共同的危机，让我们人类不得不彼此靠近，不能不唇齿相依，除了学会成为彼此一家的世界公民，学会互相之间兄弟姐妹般的友善和宽容，我们已经别无选择。

二

　　我们因此正在走向"人类命运共同体和全球责任共同体"的特殊时代，世界各国人民因此必须走出宗教文化壁垒，跨越意识形态障碍，超越政治制度边界，以世界公民的身份，与其他国家和民族的人民一道，共同承担起人类社会的可持续发展责任。我们每一个人不仅需要具有自觉的世界公民责任意识，更需要具有能承担起世界公民责任的基本素质和技能——在这样一个事关我们每一个人现在的生存质量、决定我们每一个家庭明天的

生活希望的全球性危机时代，我们每一个人都不能不从头开始，学会以世界公民的方式生存。

三

我们因此需要一个全球普遍适用的世界公民教育体系，但我们又身处多元格局的差异化社会之中，我们因此永远不可能有一部放之四海而皆准的世界公民统编教材，但是我们却可以而且必须互相参考和借鉴。我们因此倡导"互相阅读"和"比较阅读"式的世界公民教育，这本身就是一种承担共同责任的世界公民行为，是人类面对全球性危机时，首先需要的一种协商、协调、协同的智慧和行为。我们相信，尽管一方面，世界各国发展不平衡，世界各民族和地区的文化各不相同，应对全球性危机和承担世界公民责任的方式、方法和路径各不相同，但是，另一方面，世界各国无论贫富，世界各地无论远近，世界各民族文化无论有多么地不同，都毫无例外地、没有差别地、不可逃避地承受着同样的全球性危机的影响和压力，都必须协调一致，在人类的共同拯救行动中才能最终拯救自己。

四

综观世界各国的公民教育，无论是发达国家还是发展中国家，基本素质和基本技能都是公民教育的核心内容，唯其如此，世界各国的公民教育经验才具有互相参考和借鉴的可能性，不同语言的公民教育读本才具有互相阅读的必要性。

在众多国家出版的众多公民教育读本中，美国公民教育中心的一整套教材，在这方面最具有代表性。这套公民教育读本，可以说是"最高地位的社会名流邀请最高学问的专家一道，弯下腰来，以最低的姿态，奉献给他们认为是最高大的幼儿、少年、青年们的《公民圣经》"。这套由美国以及世界上多个国家多方面领域的专家经过多年精心编修的读本，没有高深的理论，没有刻板的道理，没有号称伟大的思想体系，没有不可置疑的绝对真理，而是结合人生成长的不同阶段，针对不同年龄青少年的学习、生活和成长实际，引导学生，通过自己的独立判断、反思鉴别、团队合作、谈判妥协、陈述坚持、提案答辩等理性的方法和智慧的工具，在观察、发现、认知、处理身边各种与公民权利和责任有关的问题的过程中，成长为一个具有公民美德基本素质和履行社会责任的基本技能的合格公民。

## 五

我们深知，无论多么好的公民素质和技能，离开了养成这种素质和技能的国度，就不一定有效，我们因此只是将这套美国公民教育读本作为中国公民的参考读物，原原本本地译介过来，用作借鉴，而非直接用作教材；我们深知，无论多么好的公民教育读本，离开了产生这种读本的文字语言环境，就很难领略其中丰富的意蕴，我们因此采用中英文对照的方式出版，即便是当作学习美国英语的泛读教材，也不失为一种明智的选择，因为这套读本用最基本的词汇和最浅显的文体，最准确地阐释了美国最基本的社会实质和美国公民最基本的生活真实。

## 六

《世界公民读本》（文库），是一项长期性的、庞大的公益出版计划，其宗旨在于倡导全社会的"公民阅读"。公民阅读和私人兴趣阅读不一样的地方在于，私人阅读更关注个体自身的心灵世界、个人的知识需求和个性化的审美愉悦，而公民阅读更关心的是公共生活的领域、人类共同的价值和世界更好的未来。从这个意义上来说，公民阅读是一种更加需要精神品德和高尚情怀的开放式阅读、互动式阅读和参与式阅读，也正是在这个意义上，可以说，我们翻译出版给国人阅读的这套《世界公民读本》，其实也是真正意义上的《好人读本》、《成功读本》、《领袖读本》，是每一个人，要想成长、成熟、成功的基本教科书，是任何人一生中的"第一启蒙读本"。

## 七

我们的民族是一个崇尚"好人"的民族，深受"穷则独善其身，达则兼济天下"的自我完善文化影响，更有所谓"不在其位、不谋其政"的古老训条，这些都很容易被借用来为我们远离社会理想、逃避公民责任构建自我安慰的巢穴。人们因此更愿意以"独善"的"好人"自居，而怯于以"兼济"的"好公民"自励。

尽管我们的传统是一个没有公民的好人社会传统，但我们的时代却是一个需要好公民的大社会时代，在这样的文化纠结中，就让我们用世界公民的阅读方式延续中国的好人传统，用好人的传统善意理解当今的公民世界。这可以说是我们编辑出版《世界公民读本》（文库）的初衷。

## 八

我们期待着有一天，公民这个称呼，能够像"贤人"一样，成为令每一个中国人都值得骄傲的赞许；世界公民这个身份，能够像"圣人"一样，成为中华传统至高无上的美德的代名词。

我们相信有一天，一个普通的中国人面对世界的时候，也能够像美国的奥巴马一样，以世界公民的身份向世界的公民们说：

"Tonight, I speak to you not as a candidate for President, but as a citizen— a proud citizen of the United States, and a fellow citizen of the world."（今晚，我并不是以一个总统候选人的身份在这里向大家演讲，而是以一位公民—— 一位以美国为荣的公民和一位世界公民的身份跟大家讲话。）

"I am a citizen of the world." 我是一个世界公民。你准备好了吗？

# 编者语

　　这是一些将民主与法治当作信仰，相信它能够成为社会的秩序原则与社会运行方式，并坚信理性力量的知识精英，历经数年共同精心编纂的一部书。他们满怀激情、充满智慧，以建筑一座理想中恢宏大厦的决心，做着构建最扎实地基的工作——公民教育。

　　被命名为《民主的基础》的这一辑的读者对象，是甫将开始独立社会生活的青年。这些青年，正是保证前人着力思考过、倾心建设过的民主与法治机制——同时也是具有普世价值的文化传统和社会生活信念，能够得以延续的基石。

　　作为美国高中的课程读本，《民主的基础》由《权威》、《隐私》、《责任》、《正义》四个部分构成。所涉问题常常会触碰到个体的自我面对群体的他者时的一些核心价值冲突，令我们本能、直觉的感受纠结与困扰。但是，我们都知道，这世界是由一个个独立的个体组成的一个共同体，社会共有的秩序与幸福是达成个体幸福的基础。在纷繁复杂的人际社会中、在相互冲突的利益与价值面前，必须权衡利弊，做出理性的思考与选择。因此，只有当一个社会有更多能够独立思考的人、以社会的共同利益为目标捍卫个人权利的人，我们才能够期待这个社会更加和谐美好。

　　该丛书的要旨不仅是带领研习者广泛而深入的思考权威、隐私、责任、正义这些至关重要的问题，更是通过思想智慧、知识经验给出了一个叫做"知识工具"的东西。"它是一种思想工具，是研究问题和制定决策的一系列思路与方法的集合。"运用这些工具，不仅能帮助我们更好地解析这些核心理念，更通过由理念到操作层面的分析与权衡，令研读者通过熟练运用具体的指标体系，形成对研究对象的判断与决策，在面对多重利益交叠的复杂的社会政治生活、决定我们的态度和行动方式的时候，超越情感，不是凭主观感受，而是理性、平和、有序的使用知识工具做出衡量与选择。

　　可以说，这套书是一部精粹的法治文化及公民教育领域的思想方法读本，是了解美国核心民主法治建构理念与公平公正处世方略的钥匙，是把握理性权衡与处置个体与社会共同体之间利益与冲突的工具，同时也是学习最简洁、规范、实用的文化英语和法律英语的范本。相信该丛书会从多个方面给予我们启迪。

Foundations of Democracy introduces you to four ideas which are basic to our constitutional form of government: authority, privacy, responsibility, and justice. These are not only ideas that need to be grasped in order to understand the foundations of our government, but they are crucial to evaluating the important differences between a constitutional democracy and a society that is not free.

《民主的基础》将向你们介绍美国政府的宪政模式中的四种基本观念：权威、隐私、责任和正义。理解和掌握这四种观念，不仅有助于理解美国政府的立国之本，更是评估和区分"宪政民主"与"不自由的社会"的关键。

# Preface

Foundations of Democracy introduces you to four ideas which are basic to our constitutional form of government: authority, privacy, responsibility, and justice. These are not only ideas that need to be grasped in order to understand the foundations of our government, but they are crucial to evaluating the important differences between a constitutional democracy and a society that is not free.

There are costs or burdens that we must bear in order to preserve our freedom and the values on which our nation was founded. There are many situations in which hard choices need to be made between competing values and interests. In this course of study, you will be challenged to discuss and debate situations involving the use of authority and the protection of privacy. You will be asked to decide how responsibilities should be fulfilled and how justice could be achieved in a number of situations.

You will learn different approaches and ideas, which we call "intellectual tools," to evaluate these situations. Intellectual tools help you think clearly about issues of authority, privacy, responsibility, and justice. They help you develop your own positions, and support your positions which reasons.

The knowledge and skills you gain in this course of study will assist you not only in addressing issues of public policy, but also in everyday situations you face in your private life. By thinking for yourself, reaching your own conclusions, and defending your positions, you can be a more effective and active citizen in a free society.

# 前　言

　　《民主的基础》将向你们介绍美国政府的宪政模式中的四种基本观念：权威、隐私、责任和正义。理解和掌握这四种观念，不仅有助于理解美国政府的立国之本，更是评估和区分"宪政民主"与"不自由的社会"的关键。

　　为了维护我们的国家得以建立的自由和价值，我们必须付出代价或承担责任，我们也必须在许多相互冲突的价值和利益中做出选择。在本课程的学习中，你们将会针对运用权威和保护隐私的案例进行讨论和辩论，你们将要回答在一系列情况下应当如何承担责任、怎样才能实现正义的问题。

　　在本课程中，你们将学到各种不同的方法和观念（在这里我们统称为"知识工具"），并运用这些工具来评估不同的案例和情况。知识工具不仅将帮助你们对有关权威、隐私、责任和正义的问题进行更清晰的思考，也将有助于你们形成自己的观点，并通过推理来论证自己的观点。

　　在本课程学习过程中所获得的知识与技能，不仅将有助于你们应对未来的公共政策问题，也能帮助你们面对个人生活中的日常情况。通过独立思考，形成自己的观点并对此进行论证。作为一个公民的你，将更有效、更主动地投身于自由的社会中。

# RESPONSIBILITY

## Table of Contents

# 目录

 This statue in front of the United States Supreme Court building symbolizes the responsibility of government to make and enforce the law. What might happen if government failed to fulfill this responsibility?

美国最高法院大楼前的这尊雕像象征着政府制定与执行法律的责任。如果政府无法履行这一责任，将会发生什么事？

## Introduction

> We the People of the United States, in order to form a more perfect Union, establish justice, insure domestic tranquility, provide for the common defense, promote the general welfare, and secure the blessings of liberty to ourselves and our posterity, do ordain and establish this Constitution for the United States of America.

The Preamble to the Constitution of the United States clearly states the purposes for which we, the people, have created our government. We have given it the responsibility to treat all people fairly, provide for the common defense, promote the general welfare, and safeguard our freedoms. We have given our government a great deal of power to carry out these responsibilities.

What can we do to make sure our government fulfills its responsibilities? What responsibilities do we have to ourselves and to our government? We, as citizens, have the right to determine how our government uses its power. We have the responsibility to ensure that our government protects the rights of all people and promotes the general welfare. To be effective citizens, we need to understand both the responsibilities of government and the responsibilities of citizens and we should be able to make informed decisions about those responsibilities.

What you study here will help you deal with issues of responsibility as they arise in your life. You will learn some intellectual tools to help you make informed and wise decisions about issues of responsibility. The knowledge and skills you gain will help you assume the responsibilities of citizenship in our democratic society and help you ensure that our government fulfills the purposes for which we, the people, created it.

# 导言

　　"我们美利坚合众国的人民，为了组织一个更完善的联邦，树立正义，保障国内的安宁，建立共同的国防，增进全民福利和确保我们自己及我们的后代能安享自由带来的幸福，乃为美利坚合众国制定和确立这一部宪法。"

　　美国宪法的序言清楚地说明了我们美国人民创立政府的目的。我们赋予政府一定的责任，以使它能公平对待所有人，建立共同国防，增进全民福利，并捍卫我们的自由。我们还赋予我们的政府许多权力，以承担和履行这些责任。

　　为确保我们的政府履行自己的责任，我们能做些什么？我们对自己、对政府需要承担哪些责任？我们作为公民，有权力决定我们的政府如何行使自己的权力。我们有责任确保我们的政府保护着所有人的权利，并促进全民福利的发展。要成为有所作为的公民，我们需要明确政府和公民各自的责任，针对这些责任我们也应当做出明智的决定。

　　你们在本课中所学的知识，将帮助你们应对生活中出现的有关责任的问题。你们将学会运用某些知识工具，帮助你们对有关责任的问题做出准确和明智的决定。你们在学习中获得的知识和技巧，将帮助你们更好地在民主社会中履行公民的职责，并有助于确保政府兑现我们人民创立这一政府的目标。

## Unit One

## What Is Responsibility?

---

### Purpose of  Unit

No man is an island, entire of itself; every man is a piece of the continent, a port of the main, '" any man's death diminishes me, because I am involved in mankind; and therefore never send to know for whom the bell tolls; it tollsfor thee.

John Donne (1572--1631), the English poet, penned these lines in the early seventeenth century. The ideas he raises about responsibility are not new. For centuries, people have been writing about responsibility-responsibilities to themselves, to others, and to their country.

You probably are reminded often of your responsibilities to your family, school, or job.

What is responsibility? Where does it come from? Why is it important to society? What is its importance to you?

The purpose of this unit is to help you answer these questions and to clarify and develop your ideas about what responsibility involves. You will learn to identify certain responsibilities, their sources, and the rewards and penaltics for fulfilling or not fulfilling them This unit lays the groundwork for considering the issues involving responsibility that you will face later.

# 第一单元：什么是责任？

## 单元目标

"没有人能自存，没有人是孤岛，每个人都是大陆的一片，本土的一角……任何人的死亡都是我的缺失，只因我与人类唇齿相依；因此不必去知道丧钟为谁而鸣，它为你而敲响。"

英国诗人约翰·多恩（1572—1631）在17世纪初写下了这些诗句。他提出的关于责任的观念并不是新兴事物，几个世纪以来，人们一直在撰文论述责任——对自己、对他人以及对国家的责任。

可能常常会有人提醒你，有关你对自己的家庭、学校或工作要承担的责任。

责任是什么？它从哪儿来？为什么它对社会很重要？它对你有什么重要性？

本单元的目标是帮助你们回答以上这些疑问，并有助于你们厘清和形成自己对责任相关问题的观点。你们将学习识别特定的责任、它们的来源，以及承担或不承担责任带来的回报和惩罚。本单元将为你们在今后应对和思考有关责任问题奠定基础。

What responsibilities are illustrated by these photographs?

这些照片阐明了哪些责任?

## LESSON 1

## What Is Responsibility? Where Does It Come From?

---

### Purpose of Lesson

This lesson introduces you to the concept of responsibility and its importance in everyday life. You examine several common sources of responsibility, and explore different ways people acquire responsibilities-whether they are freely chosen, imposed by others, or assumed unconsciously.

When you have completed the lesson, you should be able to identify different sources of responsibility and explain how and why people assume specific responsibilities.

---

### Terms to Know

contract                    constituents

responsibility              obligation

moral principles            civic principles

### Critical Thinking Exercise

**DETERMINING SENATOR SMITH'S RESPONSIBILITIES**

Read the selection below about Senator Smith and answer the "What do you think?" questions.

**To Ban or Not to Ban?**

Cigarette smoking is a serious national problem. Every year thousands of Americans die from lung cancer. Studies have shown a direct 'link between cigarette smoking and cancer; even breathing the smoke from someone else's cigarette has proved dangerous. The issue of banning cigarette smoking in public places has become increasingly controversial as smokers defend their rights to individual freedom and nonsmokers argue about their rights to a healthy environment.

# 第一课：什么是责任？它从何而来？

## 本课目标

本课将向你们介绍责任的概念以及责任在日常生活中的重要性。你们将研究责任的几种常见来源，并探讨人们承担责任的不同方式——不论他们是自愿选择的，被他人强迫的，还是不知不觉承担起来的。

学完本课后，你们应当能够区分责任的不同来源，并说明人们承担特定责任的方式和原因。

## 掌握词汇

| | | |
|---|---|---|
| 契约 | 选民 | 责任 |
| 义务 | 道德原则 | 公民原则 |

## 重点思考练习

### 指出参议员史密斯的责任

阅读下面有关参议员史密斯的材料，回答"你怎么看？"这一部分的问题。

### 禁止还是允许？

吸烟是一个严重的全国性问题，每年有成千上万的美国人死于肺癌。研究表明，吸烟与癌症之间有着直接的联系；甚至吸二手烟也被证明是十分危险的。在公共场合禁止吸烟的问题变得越来越具争议性：吸烟的人认为他们有捍卫个人自由的权利，而不吸烟的人则认为他们有生活在健康环境中的权利。

Senator Jean Smith represents a tobacco growing state in which the cigarette industry plays a key role. There is a bill before Congress to ban smoking in public places. Passage of this bill could cause many people in Senator Smith's state to lose their jobs. It would have a major impact on the economy of the state.

Senator Smith personally believes smoking is dangerous and would prefer that people not smoke in public. She herself is a nonsmoker. On the other hand, she is fully aware that passage of this bill would have a negative impact on her state. Senator Smith is faced with the dilemma common to many members of Congress: is it her responsibility to vote for the general good of the country or to represent the interests of her state?

### What do you think?

1. What reasons can you think of for Senator Smith to vote against the bill, even if she thinks it would make a good law?

2. What reasons can you think of for Senator Smith to vote for the bill, even if she thinks it would have a negative impact on her state?

3. If Senator Smith votes for the bill, what might be the consequences for herself, her state, and the nation?

4. If Senator Smith votes against the bill, what might be the consequences for herself, her state, and the nation?

5. If you were Senator Smith, what would you do? Can you think of a way to accommodate the interests of both the state and the nation?

6. Generallyspeaking,do you think elected representatives have a responsibility to follow the wishes of their constituents, or to exercise their best judgment for the good of the country? Explain.

The questions you have just considered involve issues of responsibility. They are difficult to answer. To make wise choices you will need some tools that can help you analyze the complex issues involved. This section of the book gives you these tools and challenges you to consider issues of responsibility.

参议员琼·史密斯所代表的州以烟草种植为主，烟草业发挥了关键作用。最近一份要求在公共场所禁烟的法案提交到国会。如果该提案获得通过，参议员史密斯所在的州将有许多人失业，这对该州的经济将产生重大影响。

参议员史密斯个人认为吸烟是很危险的，并倾向于认为人们不应当在公共场所吸烟，她自己也不吸烟。另一方面，她非常明白，如果这个提案获得通过将对自己所在的州产生负面影响。许多国会议员都面临着与参议员史密斯相似的困境：她的责任应该是为全国人民的共同利益投票呢，还是应该代表自己所在的州的利益呢？

### 你怎么看？

1. 为参议员史密斯想想，有什么理由可以投票反对这个提案，即使她清楚这将是一部善法？

2. 为参议员史密斯想想，有什么理由可以投票支持这个提案，即使她认为这将对她所在的州产生不利影响？

3. 如果参议员史密斯投票支持这项提案，将会为她个人、她所代表的州和国家分别带来什么结果？

4. 如果参议员史密斯投票反对这项提案，将会为她个人、她所代表的州和国家分别带来什么结果？

5. 如果你是参议员史密斯，你会怎么做？你能想出一个协调州与国家双方利益的方法吗？

6. 一般说来，你认为选举产生的参议员的责任是应当遵循选民的意愿，还是应该从整个国家的利益出发，作出自己最明智的判断？请解释。

以上你们所考虑的问题涉及责任问题的方方面面，它们很难回答。要做出明智的选择，你们需要一些工具，以帮助你们分析其中涉及的复杂问题。本书的这一部分将为你们提供这些工具，并促使你们考虑有关责任的问题。

**What is responsibility?**

What do we mean by responsibility? In the first three units that deal with this concept we use the word in a very specific way.

- Responsibility is the duty or obligation of a person to do something or to behave in a particular way. For example, you have the responsibility to attend school.

- Responsibility is also the duty or obligation of a person not to do something or not to behave in a particular way. For example, you have the responsibility not to steal merchandise when you go shopping.

Perhaps when you hear the word responsibility you think of having to do something that you do not want to do. You know that if you do not fulfill your responsibility, you might have to take the consequences. You also know, however, that if you do fulfill your responsibility, you might be rewarded. Typically, although not always, those who fulfill responsibilities are rewarded in some way. Usually, those who fail to fulfill responsibilities incur penalties of some sort.

We sometimes have mixed feelings about responsibility and the burdens that it may impose on us. Yet we often take for granted that those around us will carry out their responsibilities. Imagine what your life would be like at home, at school, and in your community if no one accepted or fulfilled their responsibilities. How would you feel, for example, if you had to fly in an airplane but could not be certain that the flight crew, maintenance personnel, and control tower operators had fulfilled their responsibilities to protect your safety?

### 责任是什么?

我们所指的"责任"是什么?在关于这一概念的前三个单元中,我们提到的这个词有特定的含义。

责任是一个人做某事或以某种特定方式行动的义务。例如,你有责任去上学。

责任也是一个人不去做某事或不以某种特定方式行动的义务。例如,在购物的时候,你有责任不去偷窃商品。

当听到"责任"这个词的时候,你可能认为这是要求你做那些你不想做的事。要知道,如果你不履行自己的责任,就可能要承担其后果。同时你也知道,如果你承担了自己的责任,也可能会得到回报。一般来说(但并不总是),承担了自己责任的人都会以某种方式获得回报,而那些未能承担责任的人常常会受到某种惩罚。

我们有时会将责任感与它可能施加给我们的负担混为一谈,并且我们也常常将周围的人会承担他们自己的责任视为理所当然。试想一下,如果在家里、学校和社区里没有人接受或承担自己的责任,那么,你的生活将会变成什么样子。举个例子来说,如果你不得不搭乘飞机去某地,但你却无法确定机组人员、维修人员以及机场控制塔的操作员是否能履行他们的责任以确保你的安全,你会有什么感受?

**Where does responsibility come from?**

Responsibilities may come from a variety of sources. They may develop as a result of our jobs,our school, the law, or our moral principles. Some responsibilities may come from only one source, others from two or more sources.

Nine important sources of responsibility are described in the next column. As you read about each category, think of responsibilities you have that might have a similar source. In each case, answer the following questions. Did you chose the responsibility freely? Was the responsibility imposed on you? Did you assume the responsibility without consciously thinking about doing so?

1. **UPBRINGING**. People take on responsibilities as a result of the influence of their parents, family members, and others close to them, such as friends and teachers. Obligations such as helping with household chores, taking care of younger children, and obeying family rules are typical responsibilities for many young people. Families also can pass to their children religious and moral beliefs that call for the performance of certain duties.

How are religious responsibilities and traditions passed from generation to generation? ☞

### 责任从何而来？

责任的来源可能有很多种，它可能因为我们的工作、学校、法律、或者道德原则而产生，某些责任可能只有一个来源，而有一些责任的来源可能有两个以上。

下面将介绍九种重要的责任来源，在阅读每一种来源的时候，思考一下你所承担的责任中哪些具有相似的来源。在了解每种责任来源后，回答以下问题：你是否自由地选择了这种责任？这种责任是强加在你身上的吗？你是否没有进行有意识的思考就承担了这种责任？

1. **教养**：人们承担某些责任受到了他们的父母、家庭成员以及其他亲近的人（例如朋友和老师）的影响。帮助干家务活、照顾年幼的孩子以及遵守家里的规矩等义务，对许多年轻人来说都是常见的责任。家长也会向孩子灌输某些要承担特定职责的宗教及道德信仰。

宗教责任和传统如何在世代之间传承？

2. **PROMISES.** When we make promises to others, we are expected to fulfill them, to live up to our word. We understand from an early age that a promise should be kept. That is why very young children can be heard complaining, but you promised I Promises may be stated explicitly or they may be implied. A promise may be a private verbal agreement, such as a pledge to help a friend, or a written legal contract such as an agreement to repay a loan.

3. **ASSIGNMENT.** Whether you are going to school or working at a job, others will most likely assign certain responsibilities to you. For example, in school your teacher may assign homework or give you the responsibility to develop a computer program; in a job, your boss might assign you the responsibility of cleaning the shop or managing other employees.

4. **APPOINTMENT.** In some instances, people are appointed to positions that carry certain responsibilities. For example, the president of the United States appoints people to serve as ambassadors to foreign countries; a club president might appoint a member to take minutes at a meeting. Appointments differ from assignments in that they can usually be refused without penalty.

What are the responsibilities of a United States ambassador to a foreign country and what are the sources of those responsibilities? ☞

2. **承诺**：当我们对其他人做出承诺时，对方会期望我们履行并信守诺言。我们从很小的时候就明白应该遵守承诺，这就是为什么很小的孩子也会抱怨："可是你答应过！"承诺可能是直接表述出来的，也可能是被暗示的；可能是个人的口头许诺，比如保证要帮助一位朋友，也可能是书面的法律契约，例如偿还借贷的协议。

3. **分派**：不论是在学校还是在工作中，其他人很可能会分派给你某种特定的职责。比方说，在学校，老师会给你布置家庭作业，或者指定让你编写一个电脑程序；在工作中，你的上司可能分派任务，让你负责清扫店面或管理其他雇员。

4. **任命**：在某些情况下，人们被任命担任某些附有特定责任的职务。例如，美国总统任命某些人担任驻外大使，社团负责人可能任命一位成员在会议上作记录。任命与指派不同的地方在于，人们常常可以拒绝它们而不必受惩罚。

美国驻外使节有哪些责任？这些责任的来源是什么？

5. **OCCUPATION**. Each job carries certain responsibilities. For example, an auto mechanic is responsible for repairing automobiles expertly and efficiently. A police officer is responsible for enforcing the law and protecting people's safety. A legislator is responsible for representing his or her constituents and working for the general welfare.

6. **LAW.** The legal system imposes many responsibilities on us, including the obligation to attend school, serve on a jury, obey traffic laws, and pay taxes. The Constitution-the supreme law of our land-also places a number of responsibilities on members of the legislative, executive, and judicial branches of our government.

7. **CUSTOM.** Many responsibilities come from custom. Traditions that have been followed for a long time often become obligations. Examples include waiting in line in public places, taking turns, and observing religious holidays.

8. **CIVIC PRINCIPLES.** Our society places on citizens obligations that include voting, serving on juries, serving in the armed forces in case of national emergency, and obeying the law. As citizens we are responsible for keeping informed about public issues and for monitoring the conduct of political leaders and governmental agencies, to ensure their compliance with constitutional values and principles.

9. **MORAL PRINCIPLES**. Some of the strongest obligations that people feel come from their moral principles. Such principles may be based on personal values or religious beliefs. Examples include the responsibility to treat others as you would like to be treated, to avoid telling lies, to refrain from cheating, and to respect others.

## Using the Lesson

1. While you are studying the concept of Responsibility, you should keep a journal. Begin by observing all the responsibilities you have during the next twenty-four hours. Write an essay describing these responsibilities and their sources. For each responsibility you identify, label those you chose voluntarily, those you were required to assume, and those you assumed without conscious or deliberate thought.

2. Suppose you see a friend shoplifting. Is it your responsibility to report the theft? What is your responsibility to help your friend? What are the sources of each responsibility?

3. Read today's newspaper or listen to the news on radio or television. List three instances or events involving responsibility. In each instance, describe the source or sources of the responsibility.

5. **职业**：每一份工作都有特定的责任。例如，汽车机修工的责任是专业并高效地修理汽车；警察有责任执行法律并保护人们的安全；议员有责任代表他的选民，并为所有人的福利效力。

6. **法律**：法律体系给我们施加了许多责任，包括上学、担任陪审员、遵守交通法规以及纳税。美国的最高大法——联邦宪法也为我国政府的立法、行政和司法机构的人员规定了许多责任。

7. **传统**：许多责任来自于传统。一些被人们长期遵守的惯例常常演变为义务。例如，在公共场合排队、遵守秩序以及庆祝宗教节日。

8. **公民原则**：我们的社会为公民规定了如下义务：投票、担任陪审员、在国家危难之际服兵役以及遵守法律。作为公民，我们有责任知晓公众事务，并监督政治领导人和政府机构的行为，以确保这些行为符合宪法的价值观和原则。

9. **道德原则**：人们感受最强烈的某些义务往往来自自己的道德原则。这种原则可能基于个人价值观或者宗教信仰。例如，己所不欲、勿施于人；不撒谎，不欺骗，尊重他人。

---

**知识运用**

1. 在学习责任的概念时，你应该写一本笔记，首先观察接下来的 24 个小时内你所承担的责任。写一篇文章，描述这些责任以及它们的来源。针对你找出的每一种责任，标出哪些是你自愿选择的，哪些是你被要求承担的，以及哪些是你没有经过深思熟虑就自发承担的。

2. 假设你看到一个朋友在商店行窃，你有责任举报这件事吗？你有哪些责任帮助你的朋友？每种责任的来源分别是什么？

3. 阅读今天的报纸，收听广播或收看电视新闻，列出三个涉及责任的案例或事件。在每个案例中，描述责任的一个或多个来源。

## LESSON 2

## How Can You Examine Issues of Responsibility?

---

### Purpose of Lesson

In this lesson you learn intellectual tools to use in examining responsibilities. You also apply what you learn to specific situations. When you finish this lesson, you should be able to use the intellectual tools to analyze situations and reach decisions about responsibilities.

---

### Terms to Know

warranty                          summons

Fourth Amendment                  unreasonable search and seizure

Hippocratic oath

**How can you examine responsibilities?**

Every day you are confronted with questions about fulfilling certain responsibilities. Whether it is a homework assignment, an after-school job, or a parental curfew, you need to decide if you will do what is expected of you. To make this decision, you need tools to help you consider what is involved. This lesson provides you with these tools. Different problems require the use of different tools. You would not try to bake a cake with the same tools that you use to repair a car. Likewise, there are tools of the mind "intellectual tools" that can help you deal with issues of responsibility.

 Why might it be important to use appropriate intellectual tools to analyze issues of responsibility? ☞

# 第二课：如何研究责任问题？

**本课目标**

　　在这一课中，你们将学习用于研究责任的知识工具。你们也将针对特定的案例运用所学到的知识工具。完成本课的学习后，你们应当能够运用这些知识工具对有关责任的具体情况进行分析并做出决定。

**掌握词汇**

| | |
|---|---|
| 保证 | 传唤 |
| 联邦宪法第四修正案 | 非法搜查和扣押 |
| 《希波克拉底誓言》 | |

**如何研究责任问题？**

　　每天你都要面对有关履行特定责任的问题。无论是老师布置的家庭作业、放学后的工作，或者父母规定回家的时限，你都要决定自己是否愿意做这些他人期望你做的事。要做这个决定，你需要工具来帮助你考虑它所涉及的方方面面。本课将为你介绍这些工具，同时，解决不同的问题需要使用不同的工具，就像你不会试着用修车的工具来烤蛋糕一样。特定的思维方法——"知识工具"，能帮助你解决有关责任的问题。

为什么一定要运用适当的知识工具来分析关于责任的问题？

Intellectual tools include ideas, questions, and observations about society that are useful in analyzing situations and reaching decisions. Here is the first set of intellectual tools, a series of questions you can ask when examining issues of responsibility:

• What is the responsibility?

• Who has the responsibility?

• To whom is the responsibility owed?

• What are the sources of the responsibility?

• What might be the rewards for fulfilling the responsibility? Examples include feelings of satisfaction, increased self-esteem, approval, praise, payment, or awards.

• What might be the penalties for failing to fulfill the responsibility? Examples include shame, guilt, blame, fines, imprisonment, or physical punishment.

• Is the responsibility freely chosen, imposed by others, or assumed without conscious or deliberate thought?

In the next section you examine responsibilities in the context of a town meeting. The intellectual tools you have just learned will help you answer the "What do you think?" questions.

### What responsibilities accompany your right to free speech at public meetings?

In the United States, a number of traditions govern public meetings. These traditions originated from customs practiced for hundreds of years in the New England colonies and in other societies.

Today people meet to discuss and take action on various matters, such as school problems, neighborhood crime, traffic safety, environmental policies, and national and international issues. Our tradition of constitutional democracy guarantees each person the right to attend meetings, to be considered a political equal, to have freedom of expression, and to hear the positions of other people.

知识工具是有助于你分析问题、做出决定的和对社会的观察。以下是你在运用第一组知识工具研究责任问题时，会提出的一系列问题：

- 要承担什么责任？
- 谁要承担这种责任？
- 承担这种责任是为了谁？
- 这种责任的来源是什么？
- 承担责任会有哪些回报？例如：满足感、自尊的提高、赞许、表扬、报酬或奖励。
- 不承担责任会有哪些惩罚？例如：羞愧、内疚、谴责、罚款、监禁或体罚。
- 承担这种责任是自由选择的，还是他人强加的？或者是不经深思熟虑就自发承担的？

下一个部分你们将以一次镇民集会为背景研究责任问题，上文中所学的知识工具将有助于你们回答"你怎么看？"这部分的问题。

**在公众集会上自由发言的权利附带有哪些责任？**

在美国，公众集会遵循着许多传统，这些传统源于新英格兰殖民地和其他社会沿用数百年的习俗。

如今，人们参加集会是为了就各种各样的事务进行讨论并采取行动，例如：学校问题、邻里犯罪、交通安全、环境政策以及国内外争端。美国宪政民主的传统保障每个公民有参加集会、政治平等、自由表达、听取他人的立场的权利。

The right to freedom of speech is a basic principle of such meetings. Yet, unless those attending agree to limit their talking and remain quiet when proceedings are about to start, the meeting cannot even begin. Someone must preside over the meeting and maintain order.

Certain rules are necessary for the meeting to run in an orderly way. For example, those attending usually agree that no one may speak unless called on by the chairperson. Also, those who are called on are responsible for speaking on the point under discussion and not on some irrelevant issue, such as the most recent movie they have seen or their vacation plans. People also are required to take turns expressing their views and to let others have their turns.

The purpose of public meetings is not merely to speak out, but to do so intelligently and concisely to get something accomplished, to explore ideas, or to make decisions.

If a speaker wanders from the subject under discussion, treats others abusively or rudely, or threatens to defeat the purpose of the meeting, then the chairperson may declare him or her out of order. At that time the speaker must either step down or correct his or her behavior. If such a person refuses, then as a last resort, the person may be removed from the meeting.

 hat responsibilities do you have when you participate in a town meeting? ☞

　　言论自由的权利是这类公众集会的基本原则。然而，除非与会的人同意限制自己的发言，并在大会开始前保持安静，否则会议甚至都无法开始，同时也必须有人主持会议并维持秩序。

　　为保证会议有序进行，有些规则是必需的。例如，与会的人通常都同意，在主席要求之前，所有人都不能说话。同样，被要求发言的人有责任就正在讨论的问题发表自己的观点，而不是讨论诸如刚看过的新电影或旅行计划一类无关的话题。人们也被要求轮流表达自己的观点，并允许其他人有机会发言。

　　公众集会的目的并不仅仅只是让人们发表意见而已，而是用这样理智、简明扼要的方式来解决问题、开拓思维或做出决策。

　　如果会议当中有发言者偏离讨论的主题，粗鲁地攻击或对待他人，甚至威胁要阻挠集会进行时，主席可以宣布这位发言者破坏了会议秩序，发言者要么必须退出会议，要么需要纠正自己的行为。如果发言者拒绝改正，那么最终此人将被逐出集会。

在参加镇民集会时，你有哪些责任？

Public meetings have the specific purpose of providing for and protecting the right of all people to have a voice on issues that concern them.

**What do you think?**

1. What responsibilities are involved in the tradition of public meetings?

2. Who has these responsibilities?

3. To whom are they owed?

4. What are the sources of the responsibilities?

5. What might be the rewards for fulfillment of the responsibilities?

6. What might be the penalties for nonfulfillment?

7. Would such responsibilities be freely chosen, be imposed by others, or be assumed without conscious or deliberate thought?

## Critical Thinking Exercise

**IDENTIFYING RESPONSIBILITIES**

For this exercise, your teacher will divide your class into five groups. Each group should read the selection assigned to it, complete a Responsibility Study Chart like the one on page 36, and select a spokesperson to report the group's answers to the class.

**Group 1**: What responsibilities does the Fourth Amendment place on school administrators?

The Fourth Amendment to the Constitution protects against unreasonable searches and seizures. Two questions have arisen as to how this protection should be applied in school situations. First, should the Fourth Amendment protect students against school authorities opening and searching purses and backpacks without permission? Second, what should be the responsibility of the school to protect its students from the sale, possession, or use of illegal drugs on school property?

对事关自己的问题，所有人都有发言的权利，公众集会的特定目标就是提供并保护这样的权利。

### 你怎么看？

1. 公众集会的传统包含了哪些责任？
2. 谁要承担这些责任？
3. 承担这些责任是为了谁？
4. 责任的来源是什么？
5. 承担责任会有哪些回报？
6. 不承担责任会有哪些惩罚？
7. 承担这些责任是自由选择的？还是他人强加的？或者是不经深思熟虑就自发承担的？

## 重点思考练习

### 辨识责任

在本次练习中，老师将把全班分为五个组，每组需要阅读各自的指定材料，完成第37页的"责任研究表"，并选出一位同学代表小组发言，向全班报告各组的答案。

**第一组**：联邦宪法第四修正案为学校管理者规定了哪些责任？

联邦宪法第四修正案保护人们不受非法搜查和扣押侵害。但在应当如何将这种保护应用于学校管理时，出现了两个问题：第一，宪法第四修正案是否应该保护学生，禁止学校管理者未经许可打开和搜查钱包及背包？第二，在保护本校学生并禁止在学校范围内销售、持有或使用违禁药物问题上，学校应当负有什么责任？

A 1985 Supreme Court case (New Jersey v. T.L.O.) involved a fourteen-year-old girl found smoking in the lavatory with a friend. Both girls were taken to the principal's office where they met with the assistant vice-principal. One girl admitted she had been smoking; the other, known as T.L.O., denied it. The assistant vice-principal took T.L.O. into a private office and examined her purse. He found a package of cigarettes and a pack of rolling papers which he associated with marijuana. He then conducted a more thorough search of T.L.O.'s purse and found the following: a small quantity of marijuana; a pipe; several empty plastic bags; a substantial sum of money, mostly one-dollar bills; notes indicating she had been selling marijuana to fellow students; and two letters implicating T.L.O. as a marijuana dealer.

T.L.O. confessed to selling marijuana and the state began proceedings against her. Her attorney sought to suppress the evidence found in her purse by arguing that the search was an unreasonable infringement of T.L.O.'s Fourth Amendment rights.

**Group 2**: What responsibilities of the president are described in this selection?

In the summer of 1945, Harry S. Truman, president of the United States, faced a terrible decision. In May of that year, Germany had officially surrendered, ending six years of fighting in Europe. In the Pacific, World War II dragged on. Some U.S. military experts believed that the war might continue for another year or more, at great human cost to both sides. They predicted as many as one million additional American casualties if the fighting continued.

On July 15, American scientists conducted a successful test of an atomic bomb. The success of this test set the stage for Truman's decision. He had to decide whether or not to use this horrendous weapon against the Japanese as a means of hastening their surrender, or to continue fighting in a conventional manner, in the face of the dire predictions of his military experts.

　　1985年最高法院审理的一桩案件（新泽西州政府诉T.L.O.案）起因于一个14岁的女孩被发现与一位朋友躲在盥洗室里抽烟，并被带到校长办公室。面对副校长的询问，其中一个女孩承认自己抽了烟，而另一个女孩（即T.L.O.）却否认了。副校长将T.L.O.带到一间隐密的办公室，并检查了她的钱包。他发现钱包里有一包香烟和一包卷烟纸（这让他想到了大麻）。接着他对T.L.O.的钱包进行了更为彻底的搜查，他找到了少量大麻、一个烟斗、一些空塑料袋、一笔相当数额的钱（大多是一美元的现钞）、一些她向同学贩卖大麻的记录以及两封表明T.L.O.贩卖大麻的信件。

　　T.L.O.承认自己贩售大麻后，新泽西州向她提起诉讼。而她的辩护律师认为，副校长对T.L.O.的搜查是一种对宪法第四修正案赋予T.L.O.的权利的不合理侵犯，并以此来反驳校方在T.L.O.的钱包里找到的证据。

　　**第二组**：以下材料说明了总统的哪些责任？

　　1945年夏天，时任美国总统的哈里·S·杜鲁门面临一项艰难抉择。当年5月，德国宣布正式投降，长达6年的欧洲战争宣告结束。在太平洋战场，第二次世界大战却仍在继续。一些美国军事专家认为，这场战争还将持续一年或者更长时间，这将让交战双方伤亡更加惨重。他们预计，倘若战争继续，还将有多达100万美国人牺牲。

　　7月15日，美国科学家成功地进行了一次原子弹试验。这次试验的成功为杜鲁门的抉择铺平了道路：此刻，他必须决定是要使用这种恐怖的武器以加速日本投降；还是要不顾军事专家们可怕的预言，继续以传统方式进行战斗。

President Truman chose to use the bomb. On August 6, a B-29 aircraft named the Enola Gay dropped an atomic bomb with the destructive force of approximately four million pounds of TNT on the Japanese city of Hiroshima, killing or injuring more than half the 344,000 residents of that city. On August 9, a second bomb was dropped on Nagasaki, with similarly devastating results. On August 15, Japan surrendered.

President Truman believed that he had made the right decision. Public reaction, however, has been deeply divided Truman has been praised by some for saving hundreds of thousands of lives and condemned by others for causing terrible death and suffering. Few have failed to recognize the overwhelming weight of the responsibility he had to bear.

 Widespread devastation followed the August 6, 1945, bombing of Hiroshima. What responsibilities should a president consider in making decisions as commander in chief? ☞

　　杜鲁门总统最终选择了使用原子弹。8月6日，一架名为恩诺拉·盖伊的B-29飞机在日本城市广岛扔下了第一颗原子弹，并用相当于400万磅的炸药实施了毁灭性打击，广岛市344,000位居民死伤过半。8月9日，另一颗原子弹被投放到长崎，同样造成了毁灭性的后果。8月15日，日本投降。

　　杜鲁门总统相信自己做出了正确的抉择。然而，公众的反应却呈现出两种极端：一些人赞扬杜鲁门挽救了千千万万个生命，而另一些人却谴责他带来了可怕的死亡与苦难。很少有人会忽略这是杜鲁门所必须承担的重大责任。

1945年8月6日在广岛投放原子弹带来了大规模毁灭性的伤亡。作为战时总指挥的总统，在决策时应当考虑哪些责任？

**Group 3**: What responsibilities do these quotations imply?

I often wonder whether we do not rest our hopes too much upon constitutions, upon laws and upon courts. These are false hopes; believe me, these are false hopes. Liberty lies in the hearts of men and women; when it dies there, no constitution, no law, no court can save it; no constitution, no law, no court can even do much to help it. While it lies there it needs no constitution, no law, no court to save it....

Judge Learned Hand, 1944

In Germany, the Nazis first came for the Communists, and I didn't speak up because I wasn't a Communist. Then they came for the Jews, and I didn't speak up because I wasn't a Jew. Then they came for the trade unionists, and I didn't speak up because I wasn't a trade unionist. Then they came for the Catholics, and I didn't speak up because I was a Protestant. Then they came for me, and by that time there was no one left to speak up for me.

Attributed to Rev. Martin Niemoeller (c. 1949)

**Group 4**: What responsibilities does this oath place on doctors?

The following excerpt is from the Hippocratic oath taken by physicians as they enter into the practice of medicine.

I swear by Apollo, the Physician....and all the gods and goddesses that, according to my ability and judgment, I will keep this oath and stipulation; I will follow that method of treatment which, according to my ability and judgment, I consider for the benefit of my patients, and abstain from whatever is deleterious and mischievous. I will give no deadly medicine to anyone if asked, nor suggest any such counsel ...Whatever, in connection with my professional practice, or not in connection with it, I may see or hear in the lives of men which ought not to be spoken abroad I will not divulge, as reckoning that all such should be kept secret. While I continue to keep this oath inviolated may it be granted to me to enjoy life and the practice of the art, respected by all men at all times but should I trespass and violate this oath, may the reverse be my lot.

**第三组：** 以下引文说明了哪些责任？

"我常常希望我们能否不要过多地将希望寄托在宪法、法律和法庭上。这是虚假的希望，相信我，它们是虚假的。自由存在于每个人的心中。当它在人们心中消亡时，没有任何宪法、法律和法庭可以挽救它，甚至没有任何宪法、法律和法庭能带来什么帮助。当自由存在于人们心中时，则完全不需要任何宪法、法律和法庭来拯救它……"

——法官莱恩得·汉德，1944年

在德国，一开始纳粹来抓共产党，我没有说话，因为我不是共产党员。后来他们来抓犹太人，我没有说话，因为我不是犹太人。再后来他们来抓工会成员，我没有说话，因为我不是工会成员。然后他们来抓天主教徒，我也没有说话，因为我是新教徒。最后他们来抓我，那时已经无人能留下来为我说话。"

——出自牧师马丁·尼莫勒之手（约1949年）

**第四组：** 以下誓言为医生规定了哪些责任？

以下摘自即将开始行医的医生都要宣誓遵守的《希波克拉底誓言》：

"仰赖医神阿波罗·埃斯克雷波斯及天地诸神为证，郜人敬谨直誓，愿以自身能力及判断力所及，遵守此誓此约。我愿尽余之能力与判断力所及，遵守为病家谋利益之信条，为人治病，并检点一切堕落和害人行为。我不得将危害药品给与他人，并不作该项之指导，虽有人请求亦必不与之……凡我所见所闻，无论有无业务关系，我认为应守秘密者，我愿保守秘密。倘使我严守上述誓言，请求神祇让我生命与医术能得无上光荣，无论何时皆受众人敬重，我苟违誓，天地鬼神实共殛之。"

**Group 5:** What responsibilities does the Civil Rights Act of 1964 place on government and private citizens?

The Civil Rights Act of 1964 prohibits discrimination on the basis of race, color, religion, or national origin in places of public accommodation. The Act applies not only to places of public accommodation operated by government, such as public parks, swimming pools and beaches, but also to restaurants, hotels, stores, movie theaters and other businesses operated by private individuals and companies. Violations of the Act are punishable by fines and criminal penalties, and violators are also subject to civil suits by persons who have suffered discrimination in violation of the Act. Largely as a result of the Act, segregation on the basis of race no longer exists in facilities open to the public in the United States.

## Using the Lesson

1. Choose one of the selections on responsibility that your group did not read. Read the selection and complete a Responsibility Study Chart for the selection. Explain how your answers differ, if at all, from those of the group that reported on this selection to the class.

2. Make a list of the responsibilities of a classroom teacher. Analyze these responsibilities by completing a Responsibility Study Chart for them.

3. The Nineteenth Amendment to the U.S. Constitution provides: The rights of citizens of the United States to vote shall not be denied or abridged by the United States or by any State on account of sex. Congress shall have the power to enforce this article by appropriate legislation." On whom does the Nineteenth Amendment place responsibilities? What responsibilities are imposed? To whom are they owed? What are the related rewards and penalties? Would you say the responsibilities are chosen freely, imposed by others or assumed without conscious deliberate thought? Explain your views.

第五组：1964年通过的《民权法案》为政府和公民个人规定了哪些责任？

1964年的《民权法案》禁止在公共场合因种族、肤色、信仰或族裔问题而歧视他人。该法不仅适用于政府管理的公共场所，如公园、游泳池和海滩，也适用于餐馆、酒店、商场、电影院和其他私人或公司经营的场所。违反该法将被处以罚款和刑事处罚，违法者也会面临受其违法行为中侵害和歧视者提起的民事诉讼。种族歧视和隔离在美国的公共场所中不复存在，这很大程度上要归功于《民权法案》的实施。

---

**知识运用**

1. 在上述有关责任的阅读材料中，选择一段你们组没有读过的，阅读并完成关于这一材料的责任研究表。如果你们组的答案与之前负责向全班报告该材料的小组答案不同，说明有什么不同。

2. 列出一位班级老师的责任清单，通过完成责任研究表来分析这些责任。

3. 联邦宪法第九修正案规定："联邦公民选举的权利不应被联邦或任何州根据性别予以否认或删减。国会应拥有通过适当的立法推行这一条款的权力。"第九次修正案为谁规定了这些责任？规定了哪些责任？要为谁承担这些责任？与这些责任相关的回报和惩罚是什么？你认为这些责任是自由选择承担的？还是他人强加的？或者是未经深思熟虑而自发承担的？解释你的观点。

## Responsibility Study Chart

| Questions | Answers |
|---|---|
| 1.In the above selection,what responsibilities are involved? | |
| 2.Who has these responsibilities? | |
| 3.To whom are they owed? | |
| 4. What are the sources of the responsibilities? | |
| 5.What might be the rewards for fulfillment of the responsibilities? | |
| 6.What might be the penalties for nonfulfillment? | |

| 责任研究表 | |
|---|---|
| 问题 | 答案 |
| 1.以上材料涉及了哪些责任? | |
| 2.谁要承担这些责任? | |
| 3.承担这些责任是为了谁? | |
| 4.这些责任的来源是什么? | |
| 5.承担责任会有什么回报? | |
| 6.不承担责任会有什么惩罚? | |

## Unit Two

## What Are the Benefits and Costs of Fulfilling Responsibility?

### Purpose of Unit

In Unit One, you learned to use intellectual tools when considering issues of responsibility. In this unit you examine in greater depth the consequences of fulfilling responsibility. You learn to identify the various results of fulfilling responsibility and how to classify these results as benefits or costs. What is meant by the benefits and costs of fulfilling responsibility? A benefit is an advantage to others or to the person carrying out the responsibility. A cost is a loss or disadvantage. You also learn that people with different values and interests might weigh the benefits and costs of fulfilling responsibility differently.

Understanding the consequences of fulfilling responsibility helps you decide whether or not to assume a particular responsibility. It also allows you to set priorities among different responsibilities.

# 第二单元：承担责任有什么利弊得失？

## 单元目标

在第一单元中，你们已经学会了如何运用知识工具来思考有关责任的问题。在本单元中，你们将深入研究承担责任产生的结果。你们将了解和学习识别承担责任的各种结果，以及如何区分这些结果为利益或损失。那么，这里我们所说的"承担责任的利弊得失"是指什么？"利益"是承担责任的人给他人或自己带来的好处。"损失"是亏损或者缺点。你们还将了解到，拥有不同价值观和不同利益的人们可能对承担责任的利弊得失有不同的看法。

认识承担责任产生的结果将有助于你们决定是否要承担某种特定的责任，它也能使你们在不同的责任中区分轻重缓急。

 What benefits and costs of fulfilling responsibility are illustrated by these photographs?

这些照片说明了承担责任有哪些利弊得失？

## LESSON 3

## What Are the Consequences of Assuming Responsibility?

---

### Purpose of Lesson

If you assume a responsibility you must be prepared to deal with the benefits and costs of fulfilling that responsibility. This lesson helps you learn to identify the benefits and costs. When you have completed the lesson you should be able to explain some common benefits and costs of responsibility and to identify the benefits and costs of fulfilling responsibility in a specific situation.

---

### Terms to Know

| | | |
|---|---|---|
| benefits | costs | predictability |
| security | efficiency | resentment |

### Critical Thinking Exercise

**IDENTIFYING CONSEQUENCES AS BENEFITS OR COSTS**

What happens when you assume a responsibility? There are consequences to your choices. Some of these consequences may be benefits, and some may be costs. It is important to recognize these benefits and costs in deciding whether to take on a particular responsibility.

Read the story below and complete a chart like the one that follows. Then answer the "What do you think?" questions. Be prepared to share your answers with the class.

# 第三课：承担责任会产生哪些结果？

## 本课目标

如果承担了某种责任，你就必须准备好应对承担这种责任所带来的利弊得失。本课将帮你学会辨识利弊得失。学完本课后，你们应当能够解释责任的某些常见的利与弊，并能辨识特定情境中承担责任的利弊得失。

## 掌握词汇

| | | |
|---|---|---|
| 利益 | 损失 | 可预见性 |
| 安全感 | 效率 | 不满 |

## 重点思考练习

### 识别结果中的利弊得失

当你选择承担某种责任时，将发生什么事？你的选择将产生某种结果，其中有些结果会带来好处，有些可能会会产生损失。在决定是否要承担某种特定责任时，识别承担这一责任的利弊得失就非常必要。

阅读以下故事，完成故事后的表格，然后回答"你怎么看？"这部分的问题。准备与全班分享你的答案。

**What should Selina do?**

Selina, a junior at Elkwood High School, was well liked by her classmates and her teachers. Outgoing and friendly, with a sharp sense of humor, Selina got along well with most everyone. Yesterday, the assistant principal had asked Selina if she would be willing to take on the responsibility of serving as a peer mediator in the school's new violence-prevention program. Peer mediators helped to resolve disputes between students by listening to each student involved and by suggesting ways to resolve the dispute. The peer mediator cannot require the students to agree to any particular solution, but can help the students reach agreement by discussing the dispute with them. Peer mediators are not paid for their services, but they do receive a certificate ofappreciation from the school, and their participation in the program can be helpful in applying to college. Peer mediators must participate in a two-week training course, which develops their abilities to listen, to defuse conflicts, and to get people to agree to proposed solutions. They must be available for at least one hour every day after school to conduct peer mediation sessions with students involved in disputes.

As Selina considered the assistant principal's request, she decided to list the consequences of taking on the responsibility, to help her decide what to do.

| Consequences | Benefit or Cost |
|---|---|
|  |  |
|  |  |
|  |  |
|  |  |
|  |  |

**塞琳娜应该怎么做？**

艾尔克伍德高中三年级学生塞琳娜很受她的同学和老师的欢迎，开朗、友好、极具幽默感使塞琳娜几乎能与所有人相处融洽。昨天，副校长问塞琳娜是否愿意参加有关"预防学校暴力"的新计划，并担任学生调解员这一职务。学生调解员主要负责解决在校学生之间的争端，听取争端中每位同学的意见，并对解决争端提出自己的建议。虽然学生调解员无法强迫争端各方采纳任何一种解决方法，但能够通过与同学们讨论争端，帮助他们达成一致。同时，虽然学生调解员无法因此而获得酬劳，但校方会为他们颁发证书，参与这个项目也将有助于将来申请大学。事先，学生调解员必须参加一个为期两周的培训课程，旨在培养聆听各方意见、解决争端并促成人们认可解决方案的能力。他们必须在每天放学后留出至少一个小时的时间，与争端各方的同学进行调解对话。

塞琳娜在考虑副校长的委任时，需要列出接受这一责任将会带来的各种结果，以帮助自己做决定。

| 结果 | 利益或损失 |
|---|---|
|  |  |
|  |  |
|  |  |
|  |  |

**What do you think?**

1. What responsibility was Selina asked to fulfill?

2. What would be the benefits and costs of fulfilling this responsibility?

3. If you were Selina, would you agree to take on the responsibility of serving as a peer mediator after school? Why or why not?

## Critical Thinking Exercise

### DESCRIBING BENEFITS AND COSTS

In thinking about the consequences of fulfilling responsibility, you, like Selina, should be able to identify and weigh the benefits and costs involved. Work with a study partner to read the following descriptions of benefits and costs of fulfilling responsibility. For each one, identify an example from your own experience which illustrates the benefit or cost. Be prepared to share your examples with the class.

 Benefits ☞

**你怎么看？**

1. 塞琳娜被要求承担什么责任？

2. 承担这一责任的利弊得失分别是什么？

3. 如果你是塞琳娜，你会同意在放学后担任学生调解员这一职责吗？为什么？

## 重点思考练习

### 描述利弊得失

像塞琳娜一样，在考虑承担责任的结果时，你们应该能够区分并权衡承担责任的利弊得失。与一位同学一起阅读下文中描述的承担责任的利弊得失。根据你自己的经验，分别举出一个能说明承担责任的好处与损失的例子。准备好与全班分享你的例子。

利益

**Benefits**

- **Predictability.** When people consistently fulfill responsibilities, others know what to expect from them.
- **Security.** Knowing that others will fulfill their responsibilities enables a person to feel more secure.
- **Efficiency.** Work can be accomplished more efficiently when the people involved fulfill their responsibilities.
- **Cooperation.** When people working together on a task fulfill their responsibilities, cooperation increases.
- **Fairness.** If responsibilities are distributed fairly, and everyone fulfills his or her share, it is unlikely that some people will need to do more or less than their share.
- **Community Spirit.** If all members of a group fulfill their responsibilities, a sense of community spirit or group pride is likely to develop.
- **Individual Rewards.** Rewards may include a sense of independence and self-esteem; feelings of satisfaction; approval from others; increased recognition, status, or payment; and gains in knowledge, skills, and experience.

**Costs**

- **Burdens.** It may be necessary to spend time, effort,or money to fulfill a responsibility.
- **Resentment.** People may resent an unwelcome responsibility even though they have agreed to accept it. Others may feel resentment towards someone who has the responsibility they wanted.
- **Fear of Failure.** If people are unsure that they can fulfill a particular responsibility, they may be anxious and uneasy.
- **Sacrifice of Other Interests.** When people accept particular responsibilities, they may need to put aside other values, needs, or interests.
- **Abdication of Responsibility by Others.** If one person or group seems to have primary responsibility for a task, it is easy for others not to do their fair share.

**利益：**

- 可预见性：当人们始终坚持承担自己的责任时，其他人可以了解应该对这个人抱有什么期望。

- 安全感：当我们知道其他人会承担各自的责任时，会感到更安全、更踏实。

- 效率：当参与工作的人都能承担各自的责任时，可以更有效率地完成工作。

- 合作：当一起从事某项任务的人都能承担各自的责任时，将增进彼此之间的合作。

- 公平：如果能公平地分配责任，并且每个人都承担了各自的责任，就不会有人要承担额外的工作了。

- 团队精神：如果一个团队的所有成员都承担了各自的责任，团队中很容易形成一种团队精神和集体荣誉感。

- 个人回报：回报可能包括一种独立和自尊的感觉；满足感；来自他人的赞许；更多的认同、更高的地位或更多的酬劳；获得知识、技能和经验。

**损失：**

- 负担：承担责任可能需要花费时间、精力或者金钱。

- 不满：即便人们已经同意承担某种责任，但他们可能还是会因为这不是自己想要做的事而心有不满。还有些人可能会因为自己想要承担的责任被他人获得了而埋怨对方。

- 害怕失败：如果人们不确定自己是否能承担一份特定的责任，他们可能会焦虑和不安。

- 牺牲其他利益：当人们接受了特定的责任，他们可能需要将其他价值观、需求和利益放在一边，暂不考虑。

- 其他人放弃责任：如果一个人或一个群体承担了某项任务的主要责任，其他人很容易不去承担自己应负的责任。

## Critical Thinking Exercise

### EVALUATING POSITIONS IN TERMS OF BENEFITS AND COSTS

In this activity you analyze the consequences of fulfilling responsibility. Your teacher will divide your class into small groups. Each group should read one of the situations described below and answer the "What do you think?" questions. Each group may make a chart like the one Selina made to help examine the benefits and costs involved. Each group should then share its answers with the rest of the class.

1. To bring the nation's attention to laws that unfairly discriminated against African Americans, Martin Luther King, Jr. deliberately broke those laws and went to jail.

2. Maria Rodriguez, who had been taking classes in automobile repair, volunteered to help her friend Thomas tune up his car on the weekend.

 Martin Luther King, Jr., a prominent leader of the civil rights movement in the 1960s, shouldered heavy responsibilities in that struggle. What were the benefits and costs of fulfilling these responsibilities?    ☞

## 重点思考练习

### 根据利弊得失评估观点

在本次练习中，你们将分析承担责任的结果。老师会将全班分为几个小组，每一组应阅读以下材料中的一段，并回答"你怎么看？"这一部分的问题。每组可以做一张类似塞琳娜所填的表格，以帮助自己研究材料相关的利弊得失。每个小组都应该与班上其他同学分享自己的答案。

1. 为了引起全国对那些歧视非裔美国人的不公正法律的关注，小马丁·路德·金故意违反这些法律并因此进了监狱。

2. 玛丽亚·罗德里古兹参加了汽车修理课程，她自愿在周末帮朋友托马斯检修汽车。

20世纪60年代民权运动的旗手小马丁·路德·金身肩重任。他承担这些责任的利弊得失是什么？

3. Berta heard of an on-the-job training program designed to help unemployed people learn computer skills. She applied for the program and was given a job on the condition that she complete the training.

4. The Public Issues Committee of Kennedy High School decided to sponsor a seminar on the prevention of violence among high school students. The committee opened the meeting to speakers representing a wide range of opinions on topics such as the use of drug testing and the right of the school to search students' possessions.

5. The congregation of the Community Church of Saticoy voted to establish a day-care center for children of working parents.

6. As the fighting in Lebanon worsened, the United States government made plans to evacuate American citizens.

7. Despite the warnings of environmentalists, oil companies sailing tankers through the Alaskan harbors assured the Environmental Protection Agency that the ships posed no threat to the fisheries and wildlife in the area.

**What do you think?**

1. In the situation your group has studied, who has responsibility?

2. What responsibilities did the person or groups involved in the situation fulfill or intend to fulfill?

3. What might be some of the consequences of fulfilling responsibility in the situation?

4. Which of these consequences do you consider to be benefits?

5. Which do you consider to be costs?

## Using the Lesson

1. Imagine that you are considering an afterschool job. Make a chart of the benefits and costs involved. Describe how you would reach a decision whether or not to accept the job based on the consequences of fulfilling such a responsibility .

2. Read a recent news article about a government decision involving responsibility that was made at either the national, state, or local level. Make a list of the consequences involved in that decision, and label each as either a benefit or cost.

3. 贝尔塔听说了一个旨在帮助失业者学习电脑技术的在职培训计划。她申请参加了这个计划，并以完成培训为条件获得了一份工作。

4. 肯尼迪高中的"公共问题委员会"决定举行一个主题为"预防高中学生暴力"的研讨会。委员会邀请发言者针对从药物检测的使用，到学校搜查学生个人物品的权利等广泛多样的主题，发表了各自的看法。

5. 萨蒂科伊社区教会的信众投票决定为父母都要外出上班的孩子建立一个日间托儿所。

6. 由于黎巴嫩地区战争形势的恶化，美国政府制定了疏散美国公民的计划。

7. 尽管有来自环境保护主义者的警告，航线经过阿拉斯加海湾的石油公司向环境保护署保证，这些运油船不会对这片海域的渔业和野生生物造成威胁。

你怎么看？

1. 在你们组研究的阅读材料中，谁要承担责任？
2. 该材料中的个人或团体承担了或者打算承担哪些责任？
3. 在这一材料中，如果承担责任会产生什么结果？
4. 你认为哪些结果是利益？
5. 你认为哪些结果是损失？

---

**知识运用**

1. 假设你在考虑一份放学后的工作，制作一个表格，列出接受这份工作后的利弊得失。试说明，你会怎样根据承担责任的结果来决定是否接受这份工作。

2. 阅读一篇最近刊登的新闻，内容涉及责任的政府决策（无论是联邦的、各州的，还是地方政府的）。列出该决策产生的结果，并标出每一种结果是利益还是损失。

## LESSON 4

## How Do You Evaluate the Benefits and Costs of Assuming Responsibility?

> ### Purpose of Lesson
>
> In this lesson you see how a consideration of benefits and costs of responsibility can be used in decision making. Your class conducts a public hearing on the issue of using solar energy in a hypothetical community called Gibsonville. The main purpose of the hearing is to give community groups the opportunity to express their opinions on the solar energy plan proposed by the mayor.
>
> When you have completed this lesson you should be able to use the ideas of benefits and costs in evaluating, taking, and defending positions on issues of responsibility.

### Terms to Know

agenda

relative importance

public hearing

ex officio

### Critical Thinking Exercise

**EVALUATING, TAKING, AND DEFENDING A POSITION ON THE USE OF SOLAR ENERGY**

To begin preparing for this activity, read the description of the solar energy project and the agenda for the public hearing. The instructions for conducting the hearing follow the agenda.

# 第四课：如何评估承担责任的利弊得失？

## 本课目标

　　在本课中，你们将看到，在决策中如何运用对责任的利弊得失的思考。你们班将举行一场公开听证会，主题是在一个叫做"吉布森维尔市"的虚拟城市使用太阳能，这场听证会的主要目的是让这座城市中的各个团体有机会表达各自对市长提出的太阳能计划的看法。

　　完成本课后，你们应该能够在有关责任的问题上，运用利弊得失的观念来评价、选择或者论证自己的观点。

## 掌握词汇

　　议程

　　公开听证会

　　相对重要性

　　依职业的

## 重点思考练习

**在使用太阳能问题上评价、选择以及论证自己的观点**

　　在开始准备本次练习时，阅读有关太阳能计划的描述以及公开听证会的议程。按照议程说明来进行公开听证会。

### The Solar Project

The U.S. Department of Energy, in an experimental program, announced it would offer grants to ten cities interested in partially converting their public buildings to the use of solar energy for heating and air conditioning. The grants would cover half the total cost of buying and installing solar energy equipment. When the mayor of Gibsonville, a medium-sized city in the Midwest, heard of the grant program, he asked the city engineer's office to study the subject and recommend whether or not the city should apply for a grant.

The city engineer's office found that the total cost of the project would be about $12 million. Since grant funds would pay for only half that amount, the city would have to find another source for the $6 million needed to complete the project. The needed funds would most likely have to come from increased city taxes. During a twenty-year period, however, the city engineer projected that the system would be cheaper to run and provide a small savings to taxpayers.

The engineer's office examined the effectiveness of solar energy in Gibsonville. A solar energy system works best when there is plenty of sunshine or a light cloud cover. Gibsonville usually has harsh winters with heavily overcast skies. Weather patterns during the past seventy-four years indicated that, in the long run, there should be enough days in the year with sufficient solar power for the city to save money-provided there were few variations in climate in future years. During the days when solar energy was inadequate, the old sources of heating and air conditioning could still be used.

 How would you evaluate the benefits and costs of converting buildings to solar energy? ☞

### 太阳能计划

联邦政府的能源部在某个实验项目中宣布，政府将为10个愿意用太阳能为公共建筑中的冷暖空调供电的城市提供补助，这笔补助将支付采购和安装太阳能设备费用的一半。中西部一座中等规模的城市——"吉布森维尔市"的市长听说了这项补助计划，便要求该市的城市规划办公室对这项计划进行研究，并对本市是否应当申请这项补助计划而提出建议。

城市规划办公室研究发现，实施这项太阳能计划的总花费将在1200万美元左右。因为补助金额只能支付项目花费的一半，为完成该计划，本市还要为剩下的600万美元找到资金来源。要筹到这笔钱很可能就要提高城市税收的额度。然而，城市规划办公室预计，在20年的时间里，这个太阳能系统的运营成本将更低廉，能为纳税人节省一点开支。

城市规划办公室研究了在吉布森维尔市转用太阳能的可行性。太阳能系统只有在阳光充足或只有薄云遮盖的时候才能运转良好。吉布森维尔市的冬天通常十分寒冷，天空也被厚厚的云层覆盖。过去74年的气候型态显示，长远来看，如果未来若干年的气候不会有太多变数的话，每年应该有足够天数可提供充裕的太阳能为本市节省开支。在太阳能不充足的日子里，冷暖空调的启动仍可使用传统能源。

如何评价在建筑中转用太阳能的利弊得失？

When the mayor read the city engineer's report, he decided to recommend to the city council that Gibsonville apply for the federal grant. The response to the mayor's decision was mixed; some groups supported his position while others strongly opposed it. The city council decided to hold a public hearing before acting on the mayor's recommendation. The hearing would allow interested groups to present their opinions. The date for the hearing was set, and several groups asked to be placed on the agenda.

**Preparing for the Public Hearing**

The class should be divided into five groups. One group will play the part of the city council. Another will act as the members of the city engineer's office. The other three will each represent one of the interested groups appearing on the agenda. At the end of the presentations, the city council will vote on the solar energy proposal and announce its decision.

With the exception of the group representing the city council, each of the other groups should take a stand for or against the mayor's plan. Use the instructions and background information provided on the following pages. In developing your group's position, you should consider the following questions:

I. If the U.S. Department of Energy awarded a grant, what responsibility would the government of Gibsonville take?

2. What would be the probable consequences of the city government taking this responsibility?

3. Which of these consequences would you consider to be benefits?

4. Which would you consider to be costs?

5. From the point of view of your group, which benefits or costs would be most important?

6. On the basis of your position on the relative importance of the benefits and costs, would your group recommend approval or disapproval of the mayor's plan?

When your group meets, select a chairperson to lead your discussion, a recorder to take notes on ideas to be used in your presentation, and one or more persons to present your group's position. You also may prepare posters or charts to use in your presentation. Do not hesitate to add ideas that come up in your group's preparation period.

市长阅读了城市规划办公室的报告后，决定向市议会提议，让吉布森维尔市申请联邦政府补助。然而，市民对市长的提议反应各不相同：有一些群体支持市长的观点，而另一些人则强烈反对。市议会决定在讨论市长的提案前举行一场公开听证会，听证会将允许各个利益团体发表各自的观点。听证会的日期已经确定，许多团体都要求参加听证会。

**准备公开听证会**

将全班分为五组：一组扮演市议会的角色，另一组扮演城市规划办公室的工作人员，其余三组分别代表参加会议的各个利益团体。各方陈述结束后，市议会将就太阳能提案进行投票，并宣布市议会的决定。

除了代表市议会的小组外，其他各组必须针对市长的提案表明支持或反对的立场。运用以下说明和背景材料。在说明你们组的观点时，你们应当考虑以下问题：

1. 如果联邦政府能源部批准了补助计划，吉布森维尔市政府应当承担什么责任？
2. 市政府承担这个责任会带来什么结果？
3. 你们认为哪些结果是利益？
4. 你们认为哪些结果是损失？
5. 根据你们小组的观点，什么利益或损失是最重要的？
6. 基于以上你们组对提案的利弊得失相对重要性的看法，你们组将建议市议会通过还是反对市长的提案？

在各组讨论时，选出一位主席来引导讨论过程，以及一位记录员来记录小组陈述中会用到的观点，同时再选出一个或更多人来陈述你们组的观点。你们也可以准备一些海报或图表在陈述时辅助说明。在你们组准备发言的过程中，一旦有新的想法出现，要毫不犹疑地添加到陈述发言中。

## Notice of Public Hearing

Monday, 9:00 a.m., September 24 Gibsonville City Hall

The city council of Gibsonville is holding a public hearing on the proposed plan to apply for federal funds to be used, along with matching funds, for partially converting public buildings to the use of solar energy.

**Agenda**

1. Opening remarks by city council chairperson (2 minutes)

2. Introduction by the mayor (1 minute)

3. Presentation of proposed plan by the office of the city engineer (5minutes)

4. Responses by interested groups

a. Coalition for Conservation and Use of Alternative Energy Sources (5 minutes)

b. Taxpayers' Union (5 minutes)

c. Chamber of Commerce (5 minutes)

5. Open meeting with question-and-answer period and comments from the floor

6. Summation by chairperson of city council

7. Secret ballot by council members

8. Announcement of result by council chairperson

9. Adjournment

## 公开听证会告示

日期：9月24日（星期一）

时间：上午09：00

地点：吉布森维尔市政厅

吉布森维尔市议会将就申请联邦基金以及配对拨款进行公开听证会，该基金和拨款将用于使部分公共建筑转用太阳能。

**议程**

1. 市议会主席开幕致词（2分钟）

2. 市长介绍（1分钟）

3. 城市规划办公室陈述提案（5分钟）

4. 各利益团体发表意见

    a. 保护与使用替代能源联盟（5分钟）

    b. 纳税人联盟（5分钟）

    c. 商会（5分钟）

5. 公开讨论：问答时间，参会者评论

6. 市议会主席进行总结

7. 市议会成员不记名投票

8. 市议会主席宣布结果

9. 散会

**Group 1: City Council**

Your chairperson presents the agenda at the public hearing. You also select a mayor as an ex officio member of the council; he or she makes a brief statement at the hearing and introduces the city engineer. Your group is responsible for conducting the hearing and reaching a decision on whether or not to approve the mayor's plan.

Your main purposes are to gather enough information to make a wise decision and provide interested individuals and groups the opportunity to present their points of view.

Your group should consider the issue and develop a list of questions to ask the representatives of the groups making presentations.

**Group 2: City Engineer's Office**

Your group is proposing the plan. Select someone to take the role of the city engineer. Then help develop the presentation by reviewing the facts about the proposed project. Set forth the reasons you think the city government should take the responsibility for partially converting public buildings to the use of solar energy. Include an analysis of the benefits and costs of the project in your presentation.

How can you use an analysis of benefits and costs to argue for or against taking on a responsibility?    ☞

### 第一组：市议会

会议开始前，由你们组选出的主席说明公开听证会的议程。你们组还要选出一位同学担任市长，同时也是市议会的当然会员。他将在听证会上做一个简短陈述，并介绍城市规划师。你们组要控制听证会议程，并决定是否要通过市长的提案。

你们组召开听证会的主要目标是收集足够的信息，以做出明智的决定，并为各利益团体和个人提供表达各自观点的机会。你们组应仔细思考这个提案，制定一份问题列表，用来询问陈述发言的各组代表。

### 第二组：城市规划办公室

你们组负责提出方案。选出一位同学来扮演城市规划师。通过评述你们组提出的计划的各方面情况，来完成你们组的陈述发言。详细说明你们认为市政府应当承担将全市部分公共建筑转用太阳能这一责任的理由。你们的陈述中还要包括对这一提案的利弊得失的分析。

如何运用对利弊得失的分析来论证或反对承担某项责任？

**Group 3: Coalition for Conservation and Use of Alternative Energy Sources**

Your overall position presented at the hearing should be that the benefits outweigh the costs, and you should recommend approval of the mayor's plan. In supporting this position, your group should include an explanation of the various benefits of using solar energy.

**Group 4: Taxpayers' Union**

Your group's overall position should be that the costs of the plan outweigh the benefits, and you should recommend disapproval of the mayor's plan. In supporting this position, your group should include a description of the financial costs of the project, and the impact these costs will have on taxpayers.

**Group 5: Chamber of Commerce**

Your group supports the mayor's position. You take the position that, all in all, the benefits outweigh the costs. Your presentation should include an explanation of how the expenditure of $12 million for the installation of solar energy will create new jobs and substantially benefit the local economy by increasing the amount of money available for goods, services, and recreation.

**Conducting the Public Hearing**

1. The chairperson of the city council should call the meeting to order, explain the purpose of the meeting, present the agenda, and begin the proceedings by introducing the mayor.

2. Representatives of each group should appear in the order they are listed on the agenda. Each group's initial presentation should be limited to five minutes.

3. At any time during the presentations, members of the city council may interrupt speakers to ask questions.

4. After all groups have had an opportunity to present their points of view, the members of the city council should discuss the issue and vote on whether or not to approve the mayor's plan.

5. The city council members should announce their decision and explain their reasoning. Additional discussion by the class may follow.

### 第三组：保护与使用替代能源联盟

你们组在此次听证会中的总体观点应当是这个提案利大于弊，并提议市议会通过市长的这项提案。为了支持这一观点，你们组的陈述发言中应该包括对使用太阳能的各种好处的说明。

### 第四组：纳税人联盟

你们组在此次听证会中的总体观点应当是这个提案弊大于利，并提议市议会对市长的提案不予通过。为了支持这一观点，你们组的陈述发言中应该包括说明这个提案的财政开支，以及这些开支对纳税人造成的影响。

### 第五组：商会

你们组支持市长的提案，你们组的观点是：总的来说这项提案利大于弊。你们的陈述发言中应说明：花费1200万美元用于太阳能设备的安装将如何创造新的工作机会，并最终通过商品、服务业和娱乐业的发展而极大地推动本地经济的发展。

### 举行公开听证会

1. 市议会主席应宣布会议开始，说明举行会议的目的，介绍会议议程，并介绍市长出席，正式宣布会议开始。
2. 每组的发言代表应根据会议议程，按顺序出场。各组的第一次陈述发言应不超过5分钟。
3. 在每组陈述发言期间，市议会的议员可以随时打断发言，提出疑问。
4. 在各组结束发言陈述后，市议会的议员应讨论本次会议的议题，并为是否通过市长的提案进行投票。
5. 市议会议员应当宣布他们的决定并说明原因。接下来全班可以继续进行班级讨论。

**Using the Lesson**

1. Write a letter to the editor of the Gibsonville newspaper either defending or opposing the decision of the city council on the solar energy project.

2. Read recent news articles about a bill passed either by your state legislature or by Congress. Analyze to what extent a consideration of benefits and costs played a role in the decision-making process. Make an oral report of your findings to the class.

**知识运用**

1. 给吉布森维尔市的报纸编辑写一封信，对市议会有关太阳能提案的决定表示支持或者反对。

2. 阅读一篇新闻，内容是关于最近国会或你们州议会通过的某项提案。试分析国会或议会对利弊得失的思考在什么程度上影响了决策过程。以口头报告的形式向全班说明你的发现。

## Unit Three

## How Can You Choose Among Competing Responsibilities?

### Purpose of Unit

Think for a moment of all the responsibilities you have Then think of other responsibilities that you might be interested in assuming. Add to this list the many other things you might want to do or that are important to you. Now consider how much time and energy you have.

Could you possibly fulfill all your responsibilities and do everything else that interests you? Probably not. You like everyone else, must make choices about what responsibilities you will fulfill and what other activities you will pursue.

Sometimes it is easy to decide among competing responsibilities, interests, and values. At other times the choice may be quite complicated. This unit focuses on the considerations that can be used to make wise choices among competing responsibilities, interests, and values.

# 第三单元：在相互冲突的责任之间如何做选择？

## 单元目标

思考一下你现在承担的所有责任，然后想想你可能会有兴趣承担的其他责任。再加上许多你可能想做的其他事情，或对你很重要的事情。现在，再考虑看看你有多少时间和精力。

你能承担以上所有责任，同时完成一切你感兴趣的其他事情吗？答案可能是不行。就像其他所有人一样，你必须在要承担的责任和要进行的其他活动中做出选择。

有时在相互冲突的不同责任、利益和价值观之间作决定是很容易的，但有时候，选择却是非常复杂困难的。本单元着重研究能在相互冲突的不同责任、利益和价值观之间帮助你做出明智选择的考虑因素。

 What considerations might be important in deciding how to allocate your time among competing responsibilities to yourself, your family, and society at large?

在面临相互冲突的不同责任时，有哪些重要的考虑因素可以帮你决定如何把时间分配给你自己、你的家庭和整个社会？

## LESSON 5

## What Considerations Are Useful in Deciding Among Competing Responsibilities?

---

### Purpose of Lesson

In this lesson you add to yourset of intellectual tools. You consider factors useful in making decisions among competing responsibilities, values, and interests. When you have completed this lesson, you should be able to use these tools to evaluate take and defend positions about situations in which choices must be made among competing responsibilities, interests, and values.

---

### Terms to Know

Urgency          interests

Resources        compromise

values

 Have you ever been in a situation in which you believed that you had more responsibility than you could possibly manage? How did you decide what to do?  ☞

## 第五课：在相互冲突的责任之间做选择时，需要考虑哪些因素？

### 本课目标

　　在这一课中，你们将学习更多的知识工具。在相互冲突的不同责任、价值观与利益之间做选择时，你们将考虑一些有助于做出决定的因素。完成本课学习后，在某些必须在相互冲突的不同责任、利益和价值观之间做选择的情况下，你们应当能够运用这些知识工具来评估、选择和论证某些观点。

### 掌握词汇

紧迫程度　　　资源

价值观　　　　利益　　　　妥协

你是否曾经经历过这样的情况：你认为自己所承担的责任超过了你的承受能力？你是如何决定怎么做的？

**How can you choose among competing responsibilities?**

Choosing among competing responsibilities is often complicated. It can be hard to decide what is most important. Making such decisions often involves setting priorities and seeking alternatives. It may mean rejecting certain responsibilities or postponing them until you fulfill other responsibilities. In making choices among competing responsibilities, consider these important factors:

- **Urgency.** Deciding the degree of urgency of a responsibility allows you to set priorities-to put some responsibilities before others-and to decide which one to fulfill first. For example, it would be more urgent to work on an assignment that is due tomorrow than on one that is due in a week.

- **Relative Importance.** You need to consider the importance of each responsibility in relation to other ones. For example, you might drive into a parked car if necessary to avoid running over a pedestrian.

- **Time Required.** You need to think about the time it would take you to fulfill a responsibility and the time that you have available. For example, before taking on an after-school job you would need to consider whether you can afford to devote the time required to fulfill the job's responsibilities.

- **Resources Available.** The availability of resources such as equipment, experience, or financial means is a major factor in decision making. Without the necessary resources, you may be unable to fulfill a responsibility. For example, to take on a delivery job you need a driver's license and a car.

- **Competing Interests and Values.** You also may need to consider other things you are interested in doing or other values you believe in to decide which responsibilities to fulfill. For example, you might decide not to take on an after-school job if it would prevent you from playing in the school band.

- **Alternative Solutions.** You may not always need to decide between competing responsibilities. Instead, a creative solution or compromise may allow you to resolve your dilemma. For instance, do you need to fulfill the responsibility yourself or can you get someone else to do it?

**如何在相互冲突的责任之间做选择？**

在相互冲突的责任之间做选择通常是很复杂的，人们很难决定什么是最重要的。做这种决定通常包含了设定事情的优先级以及寻找替代方案。这可能意味着你要放弃某种特定责任，或是推迟到等你履行其他责任之后再来承担这种责任。在相互冲突的不同责任之间做选择时，需要考虑以下重要因素：

- **紧迫程度**：判断某份责任的紧迫程度使你能够设定优先级（将某些责任置于其他责任之前），并能决定首先承担哪份责任。例如，完成一份明天必须交的作业就比一份一周后才交的要紧迫。

- **相对重要性**：你需要考虑每种责任与其他责任相比的重要性。例如，如果驾车途中为了避免撞倒行人，你可能会选择撞上一辆路旁停着的汽车。

- **需要的时间**：你需要考虑承担某种责任需要耗费的时间，以及你能够支配的时间。例如，在接受一份放学后的工作之前，你需要考虑是否有足够的时间能投入到这份工作中履行职责。

- **必要的资源**：是否能得到某些资源是影响决策的主要因素，这些资源包括设备、经验或财政手段等。如果没有必要的资源，你可能无法完成某种责任，例如，要从事邮递工作，你需要驾照和一辆汽车。

- **冲突的兴趣和价值观**：在决定承担哪种责任时，你可能需要考虑自己感兴趣的其他事情，或坚信的其他价值观。例如，如果一份放学后的工作使你无法参加学校乐团的演出，你可能会决定放弃这份工作。

- **替代选择**：你并不用总是在冲突的不同责任之间做出选择，相反，一种创新的处理方式或妥协方案可以让你摆脱困境。例如，你需要亲自承担这种责任，还是可以找到别人去做？

## Critical Thinking Exercise

### EVALUATE AND TAKE A POSITION ON WHICH RESPONSIBILITY TO FULFILL

Read the following story and then work in small groups to complete the Intellectual Tool Chart for Deciding Among Responsibilities on page 82. Be prepared to share your answers with the rest of the class.

### Drugs, Danger, and Political Responsibility

The drug lords sent a chilling message to the people of the small South American country: We declare total and absolute war on the government...and everyone else who has attacked us. The lines had been drawn. On one side stood the drug cartel, its leaders wealthy, armed, and without compunction about destroying all who would hinder them. On the other side were the members of the government, the journalists, and all those citizens willing to risk their lives to protect their nation. It was truly a struggle for the future of the country. Was law or terror to rule the nation?

No one had any doubts that the drug lords were deadly serious in their threats. Murder and assassination had become a way of life. In the last few months they had killed one presidential candidate, numerous judges and legal officials, and several prominent journalists. A climate of fear pervaded the country, especially in the capital city. The drug lords had proclaimed a war that extended to the families of those threatened. Public officials were particularly concerned about their children. Some sent their families to live abroad, but even that did not offer complete protection. Assassinations had taken place outside the country, in Europe and in the United States. There was no real safety for those marked by the drug lords.

High on the most-wanted list of the drug cartel was the young justice minister of the country, Elana Gonzales. Only thirty-two years old, known as a brilliant lawyer, she had taken the post when no one else would accept it.

Of her six predecessors in the last three years, two had been killed and two had left the country. She also had been threatened repeatedly and the previous week her brother had been kidnapped and was feared dead.

## 重点思考练习

### 在承担哪种责任的问题上评价并选择某种观点

阅读下面的故事，然后以小组为单位完成第83页的"在责任之间做选择的知识工具表"。准备与班上其他同学分享你们组的答案。

### 毒品、危险与政治责任

毒枭们给这个南美洲小国的人民发来了一条可怕的讯息："我们向政府……以及其他曾攻击过我们的人宣战。"这将是一场全面而彻底的战争，战争的界线已经划定：一边是毒品联盟，它的首领富可敌国、全副武装，而且将毫无愧疚地毁灭一切阻碍它们的人；另一边则是政府成员、记者，以及愿冒着生命危险保护自己国家的所有公民。这的确是关系国家未来命运的一场战争。法律和恐怖，谁将统治这个国家？

无庸置疑，毒枭们发出的威胁是极其认真的，谋杀和暗杀已经成为了一种生活方式。在过去数月中，他们已经杀害了一位总统候选人、许多法官和司法官员，以及一些出色的记者。恐怖的气氛笼罩着这个国家，尤其是在该国首都。毒枭们的宣战对象已经波及被威胁者的家人，政府官员都特别担心自己的孩子，一些人将家人送到国外生活，但即便如此，也无法提供彻底的保护。在国外——欧洲和美国，暗杀也时有发生。对于被毒枭们盯上的人而言，没有哪里是真正安全的。

毒品联盟的黑名单上排名最靠前的是该国年轻的司法部长——艾拉纳·贡扎勒斯。只有32岁的她是该国著名的杰出律师，她在没有其他人敢接受这份职务的时候临危受命，在过去三年里她的六位前任之中，两位被杀，两位离开了这个国家。她也不断地受到威胁，她的兄弟于上周被绑架，恐怕已经遇害。

Gonzales came from a well-known family long involved in the leadership of the nation. She had built her reputation on defending the law. Now that the judicial system was under siege, she proclaimed, "We must protect the law and the government in any way we can. My responsibility is to my country and its people."

Despite her public proclamations, however, Gonzales was deeply worried about the effect her job would have on her family. She was married and had three young children. She knew that she was endangering their lives every day she continued to serve as justice minister. The situation reached a climax when she received, almost simultaneously, a new job offer and word of the attempted kidnapping of her youngest daughter from school.

The call from New York came first. She was asked to serve as chair of a special United Nations commission created to examine the international consequences of the drug trade. It was clearly a chance to leave her nation and remove herself and her family from the constant threat of death.

 How might your personal safety or your other interests conflict with your political responsibilities? How could you decide what to do?    ☞

　　贡扎勒斯来自一个长期担任该国高层官员的著名家族，她因捍卫法律而树立了自己的威信。现在，在国家的司法系统遭到围攻之际，她声明："我们必须尽一切所能保护法律和政府，我的责任就是为我的国家和人民负责。"

　　尽管做出了公开声明，然而，贡扎勒斯深深地为她的工作将给自己的家庭带来的影响而担忧。她已婚并有三个年幼的孩子。她明白，只要她继续担任司法部长职务，家人的生命就会每天都处于危险之中。当她几乎同时收到一份新的工作邀请，和歹徒要在学校绑架她最年幼的女儿的恐吓时，这两者之间的冲突已经到了不得不做出选择的时候。

　　第一个电话是从纽约打来。她被邀请担任某个联合国特别委员会的主席，该委员会正是为了考察毒品交易的国际影响而设立。很明显，这是她离开这个国家，并使自己和家人摆脱持续不断的死亡威胁的机会。

你的个人安全或其他利益会如何与你的政治责任发生冲突？你会如何决定该怎么做？

Gonzales had two weeks to decide about the job offer. The prospect of a safe haven, while still working to combat the drug problem, was tempting. It would certainly help her fulfill her responsibility to protect her family. On the other hand, she had an equally strong sense of responsibility to her nation and its future. If she left, she would be admitting defeat, admitting that the rule of terror was stronger than that of the government. She would undermine the courage of all those who had committed themselves to fight the drug lords at any cost. If she stayed, she might endanger herself and the lives of her family. Which responsibility should she fulfill?

**What do you think?**

1. Review the information you have written on the chart. What do you think Elana Gonzales should do? Why?

2. Your decision shows that you consider certain values or responsibilities to be more important than others. What are those values or responsibilities?

3. Why might another person, using the same information you have considered, arrive at a different conclusion?

## Using the Lesson

1. In your journal, describe a situation in which you had to choose among competing responsibilities. How did you decide what to do? Why did you make this choice?

2. Identify an issue in the news in which a decision was made among competing responsibilities. Write an explanation of the issue involved, the decision that was made, and the reasons for that decision.

3. Assume that you have been nominated for a top position in your student government that will involve after-school activities each week. this position would look impressive on your college applications. You also have been offered a job in the local video shop that would be very helpful financially but would conflict with the student government position. Which position would you choose to take? Why?

贡扎勒斯有两周的时间考虑这个工作机会，这将是她继续致力于与毒品问题作斗争的避风港，这对她来说十分诱人。毫无疑问地，这份工作也将帮助她承担保护家人的责任。然而，另一方面她对自己的国家及其未来也抱有同样强烈的责任感。如果她离开了，就意味着承认失败，承认恐怖势力大于政府力量，她将削弱所有那些不惜一切代价献身于抗击毒枭的人们的勇气。但如果她留下，自己和家人的生命又将陷于危险之中。她应当承担哪份责任？

**你怎么看？**

1. 参考你在知识工具表格中记录的信息，你认为艾拉纳·贡扎勒斯应该怎么做？为什么？

2. 你的决定说明你认为某些价值观或责任比其他的更重要，这些价值观或责任是什么？

3. 为什么其他人使用了和你思考时运用的同样的信息，却得出了不同的结论？

---

**知识运用**

1. 在你的笔记中，描述一个你曾经不得不在相互冲突的不同责任之间做选择的情况。当时你是如何决定怎么做的？为什么你会做出这个选择？

2. 在新闻中，找出一个要在相互冲突的不同责任之间做决定的案例，写一篇文章，说明案例中涉及的问题、人们针对这一问题所做的决定以及做出这一决定的原因。

3. 假设你被提名担任学校学生会的一个组织每周课后活动的管理职位，担任这个职位能帮助你在申请大学时给人留下深刻印象，同时你在本地音像店也找到了一份工作，能让你在经济上更宽裕，但时间会与学生会的这一职位冲突，你会选择哪个职位？为什么？

| **Intellectual Tool Chart for Deciding Among Responsibilities** | | |
|---|---|---|
| Note: Sometimes questions 7, 9, 10 or 11 may not be applicable in the situation you are trying to resolve. If this is the case, write "not applicable" or "NA" in the appropriate box. | | |
| 1. What are the responsibilities? | **RESPONSIBILITY 1** | **RESPONSIBILITY 2** |
| 2. What are their sources? | | |
| 3. What are the rewards for fulfilling them? | | |
| 4. What are the penalties for not fulfilling them? | | |
| 5. What are the benefits of fulfilling them? | | |
| 6. What are the costs of fulfilling them? | | |
| 7. How urgent are they? | | |
| 8. What is their relative importance? | | |
| 9. What is the time required to fulfill them? | | |
| 10. Do I have the resources needed? | | |
| 11. What other values or interests are involved? | | |

## 在责任之间做选择的知识工具表

注意：问题7、9、10、11不一定适用于你现在要解决的问题。如果不适用，请在相应的空格填上"不适用"或"不可行"。

| 1.问题中包含了哪些责任？ | 责任1 | 责任2 |
|---|---|---|
| 2.这些责任的来源是什么？ | | |
| 3.承担这些责任的回报是什么？ | | |
| 4.不承担这些责任的惩罚是什么？ | | |
| 5.承担这些责任的好处是什么？ | | |
| 6.承担这些责任的损失是什么？ | | |
| 7.这些责任有多紧迫？ | | |
| 8.这些责任之间的相对重要性是什么？ | | |
| 9.承担这些责任需要投入多少时间？ | | |
| 10.我拥有承担这些责任所需的资源吗？ | | |
| 11.这些责任中还包含了其他哪些价值观或利益？ | | |

## LESSON 6

## How Would You Resolve the Conflicting Responsibilities in This Situation?

---

### Purpose of Lesson

In Lesson 5 you learned some intellectual tools to help you decide among competing responsibilities. Now you apply these tools to make a decision between conflicting responsibilities. When you have completed the lesson you should be able to use the intellectual tools you have learned to evaluate, take, and defend positions on how to resolve competing and conflicting responsibilities, values, and interests.

---

### Term to Know

dilemma

### Critical Thinking Exercise

**EVALUATING, TAKING, AND DEFENDING A POSITION ON WHO HAS RESPONSIBILITY**

Your teacher will divide your class into small groups of three to five students for this activity. Each group will read the story below and use the chart on page 82 to analyze the responsibilities involved. On the basis of the information presented in the chart, each group should reach a decision about which responsibility should be fulfilled. Each group should then present its decision to the class, explaining the reasons for its choice.

# 第六课：在特定情况下，如何解决责任之间的相互冲突？

## 本课目标

在第五课中，你们已经学习了一些有助于在相互冲突的责任之间做选择的知识工具。接下来，你们将学会运用这些工具在相互冲突的责任之间做出选择。完成本课学习后，针对如何解决相互冲突和相互矛盾的责任、价值观和利益问题，你们应当能够运用这些知识工具来评价、选择以及论证各种观点。

## 掌握词汇

困境

## 重点思考练习

评估、选择和论证有关"谁应该负责任"问题的观点

在本次练习中，老师将会把全班分为若干小组，每组3到5个人。每组应阅读以下故事，并用第83页的表格来分析故事中涉及的责任问题。根据表格中填写的信息，每个小组需要决定人们应当承担哪种责任。接下来，每组应当向全班陈述自己的决定，并解释原因。

**Javert's Dilemma**

Adapted from Les Miserables

by Victor Hugo (1802-1885)

Jean Valjean had been imprisoned some years before for stealing a loaf of bread to feed his starving sister. After his release from prison, Valjean became a respected member of the community under another name, He was forced to reveal his true identity to save another man who was falsely accused of being Valjean.

Since an ex-convict was not permitted to change his name at that time in France, the authorities returned Valjean to prison. He escaped and once again assumed a new name and became a respected citizen.

During the years following Valjean' s escape from prison, Javert, a police inspector, doggedly pursued him. Javert had an inflexible devotion to his duty as a member of the police force. Then, ironically, circumstances occurred in such a way that Javert became indebted to Valjean for saving his life.

Later, when Javert apprehended Valjean, he allowed Valjean to have a few minutes to conclude his affairs. Javert had time to reflect on the task ahead of him: to return a man to prison who had distinguished himself as a selfless and compassionate humanitarian and to whom Javert was in debt for his very life.

Javert was suffering frightfully. He saw before him two roads, both equally straight. But the fact that he saw two roads terrified him. He had never in his life known but one straight line. One of these two straight lines excluded the other.

### 沙威的困境
改编自维克多·雨果（1802—1885）的《悲惨世界》

冉·阿让曾经为了救自己饥饿的姐姐，偷了一块面包，因而坐了好几年的牢。出狱后冉·阿让改名换姓，成为社会上受人尊重的一员。但因一个被错当成冉·阿让的人无辜被起诉，他不得不透露了自己的真实身份。

因为在当时的法国，有前科的人是不能改名字的，当局将冉·阿让再次投入了监狱。他从监狱中逃了出来，再次改了新名字，并成为一位受人尊重的公民。

冉·阿让越狱之后的很多年里，一位警探——沙威，仍坚持不懈地追捕着他。沙威对自己的警察职责有一种不可动摇的信念。然而讽刺的是，事情结果最后变成：冉·阿让成了沙威的救命恩人。

沙威逮捕了冉·阿让后，他给冉·阿让一些时间以了结个人事务。与此同时他也有时间反思自己面临的困境：冉·阿让的确是一位无私忘我、富有同情心的博爱主义者，对沙威本人也有救命之恩，却要被自己关入监狱。

沙威备受煎熬。他看到自己面前的摆着两条笔直的道路，这让他感到恐惧：在沙威的一生中，他从来都只知道沿着一条路前行，眼前的这两条路却是如此截然不同，没有任何交接点。

What should he do now? Imprison Jean Valjean? That was wrong. Leave Jean Valjean free? That was wrong. In the first case, the man of authority would fall lower than a common criminal, in the second, a convict rose higher than the law and trampled on it. In both cases Javert must look into his conscience and render an account of himself to himself.

What he had just thought made him shudder. He had considered setting Valjean free, which was against all the regulations of the' police, against the whole social and judicial organization, against the entire legal code. On what should he resolve now? To return immediately to police headquarters and have Jean Valjean arrested? It was clear that was what he must do. Yet, he could not.

He was compelled to recognize the existence of kindness. This convict had been kind.

Javert put questions to himself, and he made answers, and his answers frightened him. He asked himself, 'This convict, this desperate man, whom I have pursued to the point of persecution, and who could have avenged himself, granted me life. Insparing me, what has hed one? His duty? No. Something more. And I, in sparing him in my tum, what have I done? My duty? No. Something more. There is then something more than duty."

One thing overruled all else for him. He had set a convicted second offender at large.

An honest servant of the law could find himself suddenly caught between two crimes, the crime of letting a man escape, and the crime of arresting him!

## Using the Lesson

1.Design a collage of news clippings, magazine articles, advertisements, and other illustrations that demonstrates competing sources of responsibility in your life.

2. Does a soldier have a responsibility to obey an order if he believes it is morally wrong to do so? Why or why not? Write an essay in your journal defending your position on this question.

现在他应该怎么做？关押冉·阿让？这不对。放冉·阿让走？这也不对。若是关押他，执法者将比一名普通的罪犯还不如；若是放他走，罪犯就要凌驾于法律之上，践踏法律的尊严。无论怎么选择，沙威都必须审视自己的良知，并对自己有个交代。

沙威所想的这一切都让他自己不寒而栗。他考虑过放冉·阿让走，但这将会违反警察局的规定，触犯所有社会与司法机构，违背一切法律。眼下他应该怎么办？马上将冉·阿让押回警察总部并逮捕他？显然这是他必须做的事情。然而，他却无法这样做。

他不得不正视"仁慈"的存在，他即将逮捕的这名罪犯就是个仁慈的人。

沙威审问自己然后给出答案，但这答案却吓坏了他自己。他问自己："这名罪犯，这个绝望的人，我四处追捕他，将他逼至绝境；他原本可以为自己复仇，却救了我的命。他饶恕我是做什么呢？这是他的责任？不，应该是别的什么。而现在轮到我饶恕他了，我该做什么？承担我的责任？不，应该还有别的什么。有一些东西比责任更重要。"

对沙威来说，有一件事推翻、支配了其他一切事情。他最后将这名已被定罪的累犯释放了。

一个对法律忠诚的人会发现自己陷于两种犯罪的矛盾之中：一种是把犯人放跑；而另一种犯罪则是拘捕了他。

---

## 知识运用

1. 设计一本剪贴集，收集一些新闻剪报、杂志文章、广告和其他能说明你生活中责任的不同来源相互冲突的案例。

2. 一个士兵是否有责任遵守某个他认为在道德上是错误的命令？为什么有？为什么没有？在你的笔记中写一篇文章，针对这个问题论证你的观点。

## LESSON 7

## Which Responsibilities Should the Court Uphold?

---

### Purpose of Lesson

In this lesson you take part in a simulated court hearing based on an actual case decided by the U.S. Supreme Court, Wisconsin v. Yoder. The case deals with a conflict between a parent's responsibility to educate his children according to his religious beliefs and a state's responsibility to ensure adequate education for all school-age children.

When you have completed the lesson you should be able to use the intellectual tools you have learned to evaluate, take, and defend positions on how to resolve competing and conflicting responsibilities, values, and interests.

---

### Terms to Know

Amish                    freedom of religion

### Critical Thinking Exercise

**EXAMINING RESPONSIBILITY AND FREEDOM OF RELIGION**

From time to time a person's responsibility to obey the law may come into conflict with his or her religious beliefs. Because freedom of religion is protected by the United States Constitution, these situations may come before the United States Supreme Court. In Wisconsin v. Yoder, the Supreme Court had to decide whether a state law requiring school attendance through age 16 could be applied to Amish families, who argued that the law interfered with and threatened the destruction of the practice of their religion. As you read the following description of the case, think about the conflicting responsibilities involved. Then work in small groups to complete the chart on p. 96.

# 第七课：最高法院应当承担什么责任?

## 本课目标

　　在本课中，你们将参与一场模拟法庭听证会，审理一桩曾由联邦最高法院裁决的真实案件——"威斯康辛州诉尤德案"。这桩案件是有关一位父亲的责任与州政府的责任之间的冲突：父亲有责任根据自己的宗教信仰教育子女，而州政府则有责任确保每一个学龄儿童接受足够的教育。

　　完成本课学习后，你们应当能够运用学到的知识工具，在如何解决相互冲突与矛盾的责任、价值观与利益的问题上，评估、选择与论证自己的观点。

## 掌握词汇

阿米什、宗教信仰自由

## 重点思考练习

### 研究责任与宗教信仰自由

一个人遵守法律的责任可能会时不时地与他的宗教信仰发生冲突。因为宗教信仰自由是受联邦宪法保护的，因此美国最高法院的法庭上时常出现类似的案例。在"威斯康辛州诉尤德"一案中，最高法院必须做出判定：威斯康星州法律要求孩子在16岁之前都必须上学念书的规定是否能适用于阿米什家庭，后者认为这条法律规定干涉并威胁了阿米什的宗教活动。阅读以下对此案的描述，思考其中涉及的相互冲突的责任，然后分小组完成第97页的表格。

### Wisconsin v. Yoder (1972)

At the time of this case, the State of Wisconsin required parents to send their children to public or private school until the age of sixteen. The purpose of the law was to provide all children with educational opportunities. The authorities could fine or imprison any parent convicted of violating this law.

Jonas Yoder was a member of an Old Order Amish community in Wisconsin. The members of this community believe that they must raise their children according to the principles of the Old Order Amish religion. After completion of the eighth grade (usually by age fourteen), Amish teenagers are expected to leave school and continue their education by working with their parents. This allows Amish youth to acquire the specific skills needed to perform the adult roles of Amish farmers or housewives. They also acquire Amish attitudes favoring manual work and self-reliance. At the same time, the Amish teenager has opportunities to deepen his or her religious faith so that he or she can prepare to accept the religious obligations of adult members of the Amish community. In this way Amish life is maintained and strengthened.

Amish children are required to attend school until age 16 contrary to their religious beliefs. How should courts balance the interests of society and the interests of groups that wish to maintain a separate way of life?

### 威斯康辛州诉尤德案（1972年）

在此案发生的年代，威斯康辛州要求所有父母将自己的孩子送到公立或私立学校，一直到他们年满16岁。这项法律规定的目的是为让所有孩子都有受教育的机会。任何违反此项法律的人都会被当局处以罚款或监禁。

乔纳斯·尤德是威斯康辛州一个老派阿米什（门诺）教会的教徒。该教会认为，他们必须根据老派阿米什教的信条来抚养自己的孩子。他们希望阿米什教的青少年在上完八年级后（通常是14岁）就离开学校，通过与父母一道工作来继续自己的教育。这能让阿米什青少年获得特定的技能，足以在成年后成为阿米什农夫或主妇。他们也会接受注重手工劳动和自力更生的阿米什教人生观。同时，阿米什青少年也有机会加深自己的宗教信仰，为成年后承担阿米什教徒的宗教义务做准备。阿米什教徒的生活就是通过这种方式得以维系和强化的。

阿米什孩子在16岁之前都必须上学的规定，与阿米什的宗教信仰是相互冲突的。法庭应当如何平衡社会的利益和希望坚持某种独特生活方式的团体的利益？

The Amish believe that their children cannot be prepared for adult Amish life by attending high school. They feel that students would be drawn away from traditional religious beliefs and occupations by exposure in high school to science, machines, and modem lifestyles.

The state of Wisconsin believes that high school Jonas Yoder refused to allow his fifteen-year-old son to attendance until the age of sixteen is important for all attend high school. In 1968 Mr. Yoder and several other children and that the Amish should not be treated Amish parents who had refused to send their children to differently from other residents of Wisconsin. School were arrested, tried, and convicted of breaking the Furthermore, the state of Wisconsin argued, suppose that state law. They asked the Wisconsin Supreme Court to some of the Amish children decide to leave their religious reverse their convictions. The case eventually reached the community. Wouldn't they be ill-prepared for life in United States Supreme Court. American society?

阿米什人坚信，上高中并不能让他们的孩子为成年后的阿米什教徒生活做好准备。他们认为，高中学生会更有机会接触到科学、机器与现代生活方式，这将使青年人背离传统的宗教信仰和职业。

威斯康辛州则认为，在16岁之前接受学校教育对所有孩子来说都十分重要，阿米什人不应享有与威斯康辛州其他居民不一样的待遇。另外，威斯康辛州还提出，如果有阿米什孩子决定离开他们的宗教社会，他们会不会无法适应美国社会的生活。

乔纳斯·尤德拒绝让自己15岁的儿子上高中。1968年，尤德先生和其他几位拒绝送小孩上学的阿米什父母遭到逮捕和审判，并被判定触犯了威斯康辛州法律。尤德先生等人要求威斯康辛州高等法院推翻定罪，这个案件最终被提交到联邦最高法院审理。

| | Yoder | | State of Wisconsin | |
|---|---|---|---|---|
| 1. What responsibilities are involved in this case? | To educate his children according to Amish religious beliefs | To obey the laws of the state of Wisconsin | To enforce its laws providing for the education of children | To allow its citizens religious freedom |
| 2. What are the sources of these responsibilties? | | | | |
| 3. What might be some rewards for fulfilling these responsibilities? | | | | |
| 4. What might be some penalties for failing to fulfill these responsibilities? | | | | |
| 5. What are the benefitss of fulfilling these responsibilities? | | | | |
| 6. What are the costs of fulfilling these responsibilities? | | | | |
| 7. How important is each responsibility? | | | | |
| 8. How urgent is the decision? | | | | |
| 9. What is the time required? | | | | |
| 10. What resources are required? | | | | |
| 11. What other values or interests are involved? | | | | |
| 12. What alternative solutions are possible? | | | | |

| | 尤德 | | 威斯康辛州 | |
|---|---|---|---|---|
| 1. 这个案件中包含了哪些责? | 依照阿米什的宗教信仰教育自己的孩子 | 遵守威斯康辛州的法律 | 执行有关未成年人接受教育的州法律 | 允许其公民享有宗教信仰自由 |
| 2. 这些责任的来源是什么? | | | | |
| 3. 承担这些责任会有哪些回报? | | | | |
| 4. 不承担这些责任会有哪些惩? | | | | |
| 5. 承担这些责任有什么好处? | | | | |
| 6. 承担这些责任有哪些损失? | | | | |
| 7. 每一种责任有多重要? | | | | |
| 8. 这个决定有多紧迫? | | | | |
| 9. 承担责任需要多少时间? | | | | |
| 10. 承担责任需要哪些资源? | | | | |
| 11. 承担责任还涉及了其他哪些价值观或利益? | | | | |
| 12. 还有哪些可能的替代解决办法? | | | | |

## Conducting a Moot Court Hearing on The Yoder Case

A moot court hearing is like an appellate court or supreme court hearing. In the hearing a panel of judges decides whether or not to uphold a lower court's decision. No one calls witnesses or argues about the basic facts in a case that is, about what happened. In this modified form of moot court hearing, your arguments do not have to be limited to the present law or be based on legal decisions that have been made in similar cases. They can be based on the principles found in the Constitution or on any reasonable position that you take.

Your teacher will divide your class into three groups. One group will act as the panel of judges hearing the case. The second group will represent the position of the Yoders and the third group will take the position of the State of Wisconsin. To prepare for the hearing, each group should meet and select one or more persons to speak for the group and a recorder to take notes. Then the class should conduct the hearing as follows:

1. The chairperson of the panel of judges should open the hearing and make sure the procedures are followed. During the presentation of arguments, Judges may interrupt speakers to ask questions.

2. The spokespersons for the State of Wisconsin should present their arguments and respond to questions the Judges may ask.

3. The spokespersons for the Yoders should present their arguments and respond to questions the judges may ask.

4. The judges should discuss the case among themselves and reach a decision. They should present and explain their decision to the class.

5. The class should then discuss the hearing, its procedures, and the issues of responsibility raised by the case.

**就尤德案举行一场模拟法庭听证会**

你们要举行的模拟法庭听证会与上诉法庭或高等法院听证会基本相同。在听证会中，由法官组成的审判团将决定是否维持下级法院的判决。在模拟听证会中，不会传召证人，也不会就案件中的基本事实（即本案中发生了什么）进行辩论。在这种改良后的模拟法庭听证会中，你们的论辩不必囿于现有的法律，或受限于相似案件的法律判决。你们可以依据联邦宪法中寻找到的原则，或你们所选择的任何合理的立场来进行论辩。

老师将把全班分为三组，一组扮演审判团审理案件，第二组代表尤德家，第三组将代表威斯康辛州。为准备此次听证会，每组应选出一个或多个人代表小组进行陈述发言，并由一位同学负责做记录。然后全班应按照以下程序来举行模拟听证会：

1. 审判团的主审法官应宣布听证会开始，并确保听证会依照程序进行。在各方代表陈述论点时，法官们可以打断发言人并对他们提问。

2. 威斯康辛州发言人应陈述自己的论据，并回答法官们可能提出的问题。

3. 尤德家的发言人应陈述自己的论据，并回答法官们可能提出的问题。

4. 审判团的法官们应一起讨论案件并做出判决，然后向全班陈述并说明他们的判决。

5. 随后，全班应讨论此次模拟听证会、听证会的程序以及这个案件所提出的有关责任的问题。

## Using the Lesson

1. Write an editorial opposing the decision reached by the judges at the moot court hearing.

2. Imagine that you have just discovered that one of your best friends has been selling drugs at school. Even though you strongly oppose drug use, you feel an obligation to your friend not to report him. On the other hand, you also feel a responsibility to the school and to your community. Should you report your friend? Why or why not? Make a chart like the one on page 132 to help you decide among the conflicting responsibilities involved.

3. Do you believe a newspaper reporter should take part in political demonstrations? Which is more important, the right of a reporter to freedom of expression or the responsibility of the media to try to preserve objectivity in their news coverage? Write an essay describing the issues involved and applying the intellectual tools you have learned, state which responsibility you think should have greater priority.

**知识运用**

1. 针对陪审团的法官们在上述模拟法庭听证会中的判决，写一篇评论进行反驳。

2. 试想，如果你刚刚发现一位最好的朋友在学校售卖毒品，尽管你强烈反对吸食毒品，但你觉得你有义务不举报自己的朋友。此外，你也觉得自己应该对学校和社区负责。那么，你应该举报你的朋友吗？为什么？制作一个类似第133页的表格，帮助自己在相互冲突的责任之间做出选择。

3. 你认为一位新闻记者应该参与政治示威吗？是记者言论自由的权利比较重要，还是媒体在自己的新闻报道中尽量保持客观的责任更重要？写一篇文章，描述这个问题，并运用本课中学到的知识工具，说明你认为哪种责任应有更大的优先权。

## Unit Four

## Who Should Be Considered Responsible?

> ### Purpose of Unit
>
> In the first three units dealing with this concept, you have been concerned with one meaning of responsibility---responsibility as it involves the duties or obligations of people.
>
> In this unit, you are introduced to a different aspect of responsibility. You will exam ways of determining who should be considered responsible for something that has happened. Being able to decide who should be held responsible allows us to do the following:
>
> • reward individuals for positive accomplishments
>
> • determine if a remedy is needed when a wrong or injury is involved
>
> • use the information as a guide for our future actions

In many instances, it is relatively easy to determine who is responsible. At othertimes, however, it can be far more difficult. In this unit, you will determine who should be held responsible in a number of complex situations. You will leam additional intellectual tools to help you make such decisions.

# 第四单元：谁应该承担责任？

## 单元目标

在讨论责任这一概念的前三个单元中，你们主要关注的是责任的其中一种含义——涉及人们的本分或义务的责任。

在本单元中，你们将了解责任的另一个不同方面。你们将学习判断谁应当为某件已经发生的事情负责的方法。这种判断"谁应该承担责任"的能力可以帮助我们做以下事情：

为某些积极的成就而奖赏个人

在涉及某种错误或伤害时，判断是否需要补救

运用这些信息作为我们未来行动的指南

在许多情况下，判断谁应当负责是相对比较容易的，然而，有些时候却非常困难。在本单元中，你们将判断许多复杂的情况下谁应当负责。你们还将学习新的知识工具以帮助自己做出决定。

 How can you decide who should be considered responsible for an accident or injury?
How can you decide who should be considered responsible for an achievement? How
can you decide who should be considered responsible for war crimes?

如何判断谁应当为一次事故或伤害负责？如何判断谁应当为某项成就负责？如
何判断谁应当为战争罪行负责？

## LESSON 8

## How Can You Determine Responsibility?

---

> ### Purpose of Lesson
>
> When should individuals be considered responsible for an achievement or a wrongdoing? In this lesson you examine a new set of intellectual tools useful in deciding such issues. When you have completed the lesson, you should be able to use these intellectual tools in making decisions about responsibility.

## Terms to Know

state of mind

recklessness

knowledge of probable consequences

intent

carelessness

control or choice

## Critical Thinking Exercise

### EVALUATING INFORMATION TO DETERMINE RESPONSIBILITY

We often are quick to accuse or praise someone by saying, Well, you did it. It's your responsibility. What do we really mean? How can you decide who should be considered responsible?

Read the two stories below. One involves holding someone responsible for an injury and the other concerns giving credit for an achievement. In both cases, we want to determine who is responsible,

# 第八课：如何明确责任?

## 本课目标

　　我们应当在什么时候判断个人对某项成就或某个错误负责？在本课中，你们将研究一组新的知识工具，有助于判断此类问题。学完本课后，你们应当能够运用这些知识工具做出有关责任的决定。

## 掌握词汇

| | |
|---|---|
| 精神状态 | 故意 |
| 鲁莽 | 粗心 |
| 了解可能产生的结果 | 控制或选择 |

## 重点思考练习

### 评估信息以判定责任

　　我们通常在急于谴责或表扬某人的时候会说："哦，这是你做的！这是你的功劳！（哦，这是你干的！这是你的责任！）"我们真正想表达什么意思？你们如何判断谁应该为一件事负责？

　　阅读下面两篇故事，其中一个是关于认为某人应该对某个伤害事件负责，另一个故事关注的是为某项成就而鼓励表扬某人。在这两种情况中，我们都需要判断谁是事情的责任人。

**Who is responsible for the accident?**

Early one morning Charlotte was driving her small sports car down a narrow residential street. Just then George backed his station wagon out of his driveway into the path of the sports car. He could not see the oncoming car, because a large moving van parked on the street blocked his vision. A cat running across the road distracted Charlotte who did not notice the station wagon until it was too late. The cars crashed.

**What do you think?**

1. Who, if anyone, should be held responsible for the collision?

2. Is there a general agreement among class members on the answer?

3. How should one decide such issues?

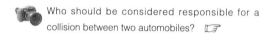 Who should be considered responsible for a collision between two automobiles? ☞

**谁应为事故负责?**

一天清晨,夏洛特在一条狭窄的居民区街道上开着她的小跑车。刚好在这个时候,乔治正在将自己的旅行车倒出车库。因为有辆搬家大卡车停在路边,挡住了他的视线,因此乔治并没有看见正往他倒车的方向开过来的跑车。与此同时,有只猫正好穿过马路,转移了夏洛特的视线,她也没有及时注意到正在倒车出库的旅行车。结果,两辆车相撞了。

**你怎么看?**

1. 如果有人需要为这次撞车负责的话,谁是责任人?
2. 班上的同学们对上述问题的答案普遍一致吗?
3. 人们应该怎么判定此类问题?

两辆车相撞,谁应为此负责?

**Who deserves credit for finding a cure?**

For the past several decades, scientists all over the world have been working on a cure for cancer. Slowly, they are making progress. Much of it is due to the exchange of ideas among scientists who report on their progress their successes and failures-through correspondence, articles in professional journals, and presentations at meetings and conventions. Step by step, the medical field is getting closer to a solution. Each advance is built on the experiences of individual scientists and their combined knowledge of the work of others. When the cure or cures are finally discovered, those held responsible will receive a great deal of credit, along with public praise and financial rewards.

**What do you think?**

Given a situation in which a greatnumber of scientists have worked for many decades searching for a solution, how can we decide who is responsible for finally finding a cure for cancer?

If you were on the Nobel Prize committee and wished to give a prize to those who found a cure for cancer, how would you reach a fair decision?

 Which member of a scientific team should be considered responsible for an important medical discovery?  ☞

### 谁应为发现治疗方法而受到嘉奖？

在过去几十年里，全世界的科学家都致力于发现癌症的治疗方法。这项事业虽然进展缓慢，但这些进展很大程度上要归功于科学家之间观点的交流，他们往往通过信件联系，在专业期刊发表文章以及在各种学术会议上做报告等方式汇报自己的进展（无论成功还是失败）。医学界正在一步步地接近最终的解决方案。每一次进步都建立在科学家个人的经验，以及他们对其他人工作的综合知识的基础之上。当最终发现一种或多种治疗方法时，对此发现负责任和有贡献的科学家将获得许多嘉奖，同时也赢得公众的赞扬和经济上的回报。

### 你怎么看？

1. 假设许许多多的科学家工作数十年，试图找到某种治疗方案，在这种情况下我们应该怎么判定谁才是最终发现癌症疗法的责任人？

2. 如果你是诺贝尔奖委员会的一员，并要将诺贝尔医学奖项授予发现癌症疗法的某个科学家，你将如何做出公平的抉择？

科研小组中的哪位成员应被视为某项重要医学发现的责任人？

**What intellectual tools are useful in determining responsibility?**

Every day people in your school, community, and government face problems of deciding who should be considered responsible for one thing or another. Sometimes such decisions are easy to make, but in certain situations, reaching reasonable and fair decisions can be more difficult.

The following intellectual tools can help you decide in a systematic, thoughtful way who is responsible for something that happened. The first three tools will help you to make reasoned decisions about when persons should be considered responsible for a situation. All seven tools should be used when you want to determine responsibility for some wrongdoing.

1. What is the event or situation for which someone might be considered responsible?

A good first step in detennining responsibility is to identify the event or situation.

For example: An event or situation for which you might want to determine responsibility could be the following:

• an automobile accident

• the discovery of a cure for a disease

• the soccer team winning the state championship

• vandalism at a school

2. Who are the people involved who might be considered responsible for what happened?

Once you have identified the event or situation, you can list the people who might be responsible for the event or situation.

For example: The people who might be considered responsible for the automobile accident described at the beginning of this lesson would be the following:

• Charlotte

• George

• the person who parked the moving van

• the cat's owner

**哪些知识工具有助于判定责任？**

每天，人们在学校、社区和政府机构中都会面临这样的问题：谁应当为这件或那件事负责？有时候做这种判定很容易，但在某些情况下，做出合理而公平的判断却非常困难。

以下知识工具可以帮助你们以一种系统的、深思熟虑的方式来决定谁应当为某件已经发生的事情负责。前三项工具将有助于你们合理地判定某人应当为某种情况负责。而当你们想要为某些错误追究责任时，必须用到所有七项知识工具。

1. 需要有人承担责任的事件或事情是什么？

   判断责任的第一步，是确认事件或情况本身。

   例如：你需要判定责任的事件或情况可能是：
   - 一起交通事故
   - 发现某种疾病的治疗方法
   - 足球队赢得了州冠军
   - 学校里发生的故意破坏公物事件

2. 事件中涉及了哪些人可能要对已发生的事情负责？

   一旦明确了具体事件或事情，你可以列出可能需要为这起事件或事情负责的人的名单。

   例如：本课开头描述的那起撞车事故中，以下这些人有可能要为事故负责：
   - 夏洛特
   - 乔治
   - 将搬家大卡车停靠路边的人
   - 猫的主人

3. How might each person be considered to have caused the event or situation?

Once you have listed all the people who might be considered responsible for an event or situation, you need to evaluate how each person's conduct contributed to or caused the event or situation. That is, was the person's conduct one of the main reasons the event or situation happened? Or would the event or situation have happened even if the person had acted differently?

For example: You might say the automobile accident described at the beginning of this lesson was caused or contributed to by the following:

• Charlotte, because she did not keep her eyes on the road

• George, because he backed out of his driveway without making sure the road was clear

• the person who parked the moving van, because the van blocked George's view of the road

• the person who let the cat out, because the cat distracted Charlotte's attention

4. Did the person's conduct violate or fail to fulfill a duty or obligation he or she had?

Once you have determined how each person's conduct contributed to or caused the event or situation, you should evaluate whether or not the person had a duty or obligation to act differently. That is, did the person fail to fulfill a duty or obligation and, therefore, was the person guilty of wrong doing or was the person acting within his or her rights?

For example: In connection with the automobile accident described at the beginning of this lesson

• Charlotte may have violated an obligation to drive carefully and safely

• George violated an obligation to yield the right of way when entering a street

• the person who parked the moving van did not violate a duty or obligation unless he or she parked the van illegally or carelessly in a dangerous position

3. 如何认定某个人导致了事件或情况的发生？

　　在列出可能要为某个事件或事情负责的所有人之后，你需要评估每个人的行为如何促成或导致了这一事件或情况。也就是说，这个人的行为是不是这一事件或情况发生的主要原因之一？或者即使这个人用不同的行为方式，这一事件或情况依然会发生？

　　例如：你可能会说，以下这些人促成或导致了本课开头描述的那起事故：

　　　·夏洛特，因为她没有集中精力看路
　　　·乔治，因为他在没有确认道路安全的情况下就倒车出车道
　　　·把搬家大卡车停靠路边的人，因为卡车阻挡了乔治看路的视线
　　　·将猫放出来的猫主人，因为猫分散了夏洛特的注意

4. 这个人的行为是否违背了自己的责任，或者是否未能履行自己的责任？

　　当判定某个人的行为如何促成或导致了事件或事情发生后，你应该评估这个人是否本来有义务或责任以另一种方式行事。也就是说，这个人是不是没能履行自己的责任或义务，才因此要对这个错误负责？还有，这个人的行动是否是在自己的权利范围内？

　　例如：联系思考本课开头描述的事故：
　　　·夏洛特可能违反了要小心安全驾驶的义务
　　　·乔治倒车进入主路的时候违反了避让路权的义务（译者注：倒车出库的车辆应让路给正常行驶的车辆）
　　　·将搬家大卡车停靠在路边的人并没有违反自己的责任或义务，除非他非法或粗心地将卡车停靠在一个危险的位置上

• the person who let the cat out did not violate a duty or obligation, since cats are not required to be kept inside or on leashes

5. What was the individual's state of mind in causing the event or situation?

To answer this question, consider the following points:

• Intent. Did the person or persons intentionally or deliberately cause the event or situation? That is, did they act on purpose? For example, a driver who purposely runs another car off the road.

• Recklessness. Was the person who caused the event reckless? Recklessness means deliberately ignoring obvious risks of serious harm. For example, speeding at 60 miles per hour on a busy city street.

• Carelessness. Was the person who caused the event careless or negligent? Carelessness (or negligence) means not paying sufficient attention to risks of harm or damage that should have been foreseen. It is the failure to use reasonable care to avoid injury to yourself or others. For example, leaving a small child unattended next to a pool or lake.

• Knowledge of probable consequences. Did the person or persons know (or should they have known) the probable results of their actions? Knowledge of probable consequences means being aware of the sorts of things that are likely to happen as a result of what you do.

Why should we examine state of mind in determining responsibility? A person's state of mind can make a difference in how we evaluate their conduct.

For example: Fred caused an automobile accident. Does it make a difference if he crashed into the other car:

• on purpose (acted with intent),

• because he was drunk (acted recklessly), or

• because he failed to notice a stop sign (acted carelessly)?

For example: Katrina set fire to the drapes with a cigarette lighter. The entire house burned to the ground. Does the following make a difference:

• she was only two years old (acted with no knowledge of probable consequences),

· 把猫放出来的猫主人也没有违反自己的责任或义务，因为并没有法律规定要把猫关在家里或者系上皮带；

5. 当某个人的行为导致某个事件或事情发生时，这个人的精神状态如何？

要回答这个问题，需要思考以下几点：

**故意：** 这个人（这些人）是有意或存心导致了事件或事情的发生吗？换句话说，他们是故意这样做的吗？例如，一位司机驾车蓄意撞向另一辆车。

**鲁莽：** 是因为这个人鲁莽的行为导致了事件的发生吗？鲁莽的意思是明明会造成严重伤害，却故意忽视这种危险。例如，在繁忙拥挤的城市街道上以60英里/小时的速度行驶。

**粗心：** 是因为这个人的粗心或者疏忽导致了事件的发生吗？粗心或者疏忽的意思是对于本来可以预见到的伤害或破坏的危险，却没有给予足够的注意。也就是说，没有用适度合理的谨慎和关注避免对自己或他人造成伤害。例如，让年幼的孩子在无人照看的情况下待在池塘或湖泊边。

**了解可能产生的结果：** 这个人（这些人）知道或原本应该知道自己的行为可能产生的结果吗？"了解可能产生的结果"意味着知道自己的行为很可能导致哪类事情发生。

在判定责任的时候，为什么我们应当考察责任人的精神状态？因为责任人的精神状态会影响我们如何评估他们的行为。

例如：弗雷德导致了一场车祸。在他驾车撞向另一辆车的时候，以下不同的精神状态是否会让他的行为产生不同的结果？

· 蓄谋（故意）

· 因为他醉酒驾驶（鲁莽）

· 因为他没有注意到红灯（粗心）

例如：卡特里娜用打火机点燃了窗帘，整栋房子烧成了灰烬。以下不同的精神状态是否会让她的行为产生不同的结果？

· 她只有2岁（行动时不了解可能产生的结果）

- she was ten years old, and thought she could put the fire out (acted recklessly with knowledge of probable consequences), or

- she was thirty years old, and hoped to collect insurance money from the fire (acted intentionally, with knowledge of probable consequences)?

6. Did the person or persons have control over their actions? Did they have a choice to do something other than what they did? Without control or choice, a person usually cannot be held responsible for his or her conduct.

For example: Juanita walked into the bank to deposit her paycheck. A group of masked robbers came in, robbed the bank, put a gun to Juanita's back, and forced her to drive the getaway car.

For example: While walking down the stairs at school, George bumped Avi. As Avi fell, he could not avoid hitting Susan, who then fell and injured her ankle.

7. Did the person or persons have more important values, interests, or responsibilities that caused them to act as they did? Sometimes important values, interests, and responsibilities justify or excuse conduct for which a person might be held responsible.

For example: Juan broke down his neighbor's door to save three children from a fire.

For example: When the fire broke out in the theater, an usher knocked out a hysterical man who had begun to shout, then calmly directed the audience to leave by the exits.

## Critical Thinking Exercise

### APPLYING INTELLECTUAL TOOLS TO DETERMINE RESPONSIBILITY

Applying the intellectual tools you have just learned is not always as easy as it might seem. How would you apply them in the following imaginary situation to determine who should be held responsible?

- 她10岁，但认为自己可以把火扑灭（了解可能产生的结果，但行事鲁莽）
- 她30岁，想通过火灾获得保险金（了解可能产生的结果，但故意这么做）

6. 这个人（这些人）是否控制了自己的行为？他们是否还有不同于自己现有行为的选择？

　　如果无法控制自己的行为，或是在没有其他选择的情况下，一个人通常不应为自己的行为负责。

　　例如：华妮塔走进银行存工资时，一伙蒙面劫匪闯进银行抢劫。他们用一把枪抵住华妮塔的后背，强迫她驾车帮助他们逃走。

　　例如：在学校下楼梯时，乔治撞倒了艾维，艾维跌下楼梯的时候又无法躲避地撞到了苏珊，结果害苏珊也跌倒了并扭伤了脚踝。

7. 是否有更重要的价值观、利益或责任驱使这个人（这些人）这样做？

　　有时候，重要的价值观、利益和责任可以为可能要承担责任的个人行为进行辩护或开脱。

　　例如：邻居家着火了，胡安砸坏了邻居家的门，是因为要救被困在里面的三个小孩。

　　例如：当某个剧院发生火灾时，剧院的招待员打昏了一个歇斯底里大声尖叫的人，然后冷静地引导剧院观众从安全出口逃生。

## 重点思考练习

### 运用知识工具来判定责任

　　要运用你刚才学到的知识工具并不总是像看起来那么容易。在以下的虚构场景中，你会如何运用这些知识工具来判定谁应该对此事负责？

**The Accident**

Peter, Mario, and Marty looked older than they were. The three high school seniors played in a band they called Marley's Ghost; they played well enough to get gigs at local nightclubs. Although the state's minimum drinking age was 18, these 17-year-old students had no trouble buying drinks with their fake IDs.

After a particularly energetic performance at the Ace of Clubs one Friday night, Peter, Mario, and Marty stayed at the bar drinking beer for an hour or two. As they stumbled to the van at two-thirty in the morning, Marty said, "I don't think I should drive. I've had too much to drink." But Peter replied "Come off it. You're okay. Besides, Mario and I have had just as much as you. Just take it easy on the road, and we'll be home before you know it."

The three young men climbed into the van, with Marty behind the wheel, Peter in the passenger seat, and Mario passed out in the back. The short drive home was never completed. Swerving to avoid an oncoming car, Marty lost control of the van and crashed into a huge oak tree by the side of the road. Fortunately, he had his seatbelt on, and merely suffered a concussion and some cuts and bruises. Mario was not so lucky. He was thrown into the back of the front seats, separating his shoulder and seriously injuring his back. With therapy, he should recover most of his prior mobility, although he can expect back pain for the rest of his life. Peter, however, will not have to deal with any pain in the future. He was thrown through the windshield into the tree, and his injuries were fatal. He died before the ambulance arrived to take the victims to the hospital.

### 事故

彼得、马里奥和马蒂看起来比他们的实际年龄要老，这三个高年级的高中生组建了一支他们自己命名为"马利的鬼魂"的乐队。他们的表演不错，并得以在当地的表演场所驻唱。尽管州法律规定最低饮酒年龄是18岁，这些17岁的学生却可以毫不费力地用假身份证买到酒。

周五的晚上，在梅花A酒吧结束了一场激情四溢的演出之后，彼得、马里奥和马蒂待在酒吧里喝了一到两个小时的啤酒。当他们在凌晨两点半醉醺醺地走出酒吧打算开车的时候，马蒂说："我觉得我不能开车，我喝的太多了。"但彼得说："得了吧，你可以的。更何况，我和马里奥跟你喝的一样多，放轻松点儿，一不留神我们就都到家了。"

这三个年轻人爬进了汽车，马蒂开车，彼得坐在副驾驶座上，马里奥在后座昏睡。但这条回家的路程却未能顺利走完。为了躲避一辆迎面驶来的汽车，马蒂急忙打方向盘转弯，车子失控撞上了路边的一棵大橡树。幸运的是，他系着安全带，仅仅有一些脑震荡和皮外伤。马里奥却没有这么走运，他撞向前排座椅的椅背，肩膀脱臼，脊背受了重伤。经过治疗，肢体的主要活动能力大部分得以恢复，但可以预见的是，他的后半生将不得不一直忍受背部的疼痛。而彼得在未来却不必面临任何痛楚了：他被抛出了车子，摔到了树上，造成了致命伤，在救护车赶来带他们去医院前，他就死了。

## Using the Lesson

1. Working with your teacher, invite an attorney or judge to visit the class and discuss what he or she takes into account in determining responsibility.

2. Working with. your teacher, arrange to visit a courtroom to observe a trial. Is the trial an attempt to determine responsibility for an event or situation? What is the event or situation being considered? Which of the intellectual tools seem to be important in the trial? Report your findings to the class.

3. Imagine you are a member of the committee selecting the student for the "Community Leadership Award" at your school. What criteria would you use to decide who was responsible for making the greatest contribution to school spirit? Write a short essay in your journal describing how you would make your selection.

**知识运用**

1. 和你们的老师一起，邀请一位律师或法官，来班上和同学们一起讨论他在判定责任时会考虑哪些因素？

2. 和你们的老师一起，去法庭参观并旁听一场审判。这场审判是否要为某个事件或事情判定责任？被审判的事件或事情是什么？在审判中运用了哪个知识工具？向全班报告你的发现。

3. 假设你是学校"优秀社团领袖奖"评审委员会中的评审员，你会用什么标准来判定谁是为学校团队精神做出最大贡献的责任人？在你的笔记中写一篇文章，描述你会如何做出选择。

## LESSON 9

## Who Should Be Held Responsible for the Oil Spill?

---

### Purpose of Lesson

In Lesson 8 you learned to use some intellectual tools to help you determine responsibility. In this lesson you use these tools in a specific situation. When you have completed the lesson, you should be able to explain how you used the intellectual tools to decide who should be considered responsible.

---

### Critical Thinking Exercise

**IDENTIFYING WHO IS RESPONSIBLE**

Your teacher will divide your class into small groups of three to five students for this activity. Each group should read the story, "The Wreck of the Exxon Valdez," and complete the chart that follows the lesson.

Each group should develop a position on who should be considered responsible for the damage caused by the crash of the oil tanker. Each group should then present its report to the class. At the conclusion of the group reports, class members should analyze and evaluate the positions taken by each group.

**The Wreck of the Exxon Valdez**

The facts of the grounding of the Exxon Valdez on March 24, 1989 have been fairly well documented. The tanker ran aground shortly after midnight on a well-charted, well-marked reef about 25 miles from the Trans-Alaska Pipeline terminal at Valdez. The tanker lost about 11 million gallons of North Slope crude oil from its tanks. The state and federal governments agree that the on-the-water response by industry was slow and inadequate. Cleanup on all or part of nearly 1,300 miles of Alaska shoreline continued from 1989 through June 1992.

# 第九课：谁应该为"漏油事件"负责？

## 本课目标

在第八课中，你们学会了运用知识工具来帮助自己判定责任。在这一课中，你们将在某个具体案例中运用这些工具。完成本课学习后，你们应该能够解释自己是如何运用这些知识工具来判定责任人的。

## 重点思考练习

### 辨清谁负有责任

老师会把全班分为若干个3到5个人的小组以完成此次练习。每个小组应该阅读这篇故事——"埃克森·瓦尔迪兹号的沉没"，并完成本课后面的表格。

对这场油轮失事所导致的灾难中谁应该为此负责的问题，各组应选择一种观点，并向全班进行陈述发言。在小组发言结束后，全班同学应该一起分析并评估每组所选择的观点。

### 埃克森·瓦尔迪兹号的沉没

大量详尽的记载为我们完整描述了1989年3月24日埃克森·瓦尔迪兹号的触礁事件。这艘油轮在进入午夜后不久撞上了一处在地图上有清楚标识的礁石，这块礁石离瓦尔迪兹的阿拉斯加输油站有25英里。油轮的油箱泄露了大约1100万加仑北坡原油。州政府与联邦政府一致认为此次事件当中，运油公司的海上抢救措施太过迟缓且不足，导致对阿拉斯加海岸线近1300英里的全面或部分清理工作从1989年一直持续到1992年6月。

The ship left port at 9 p.m. on March 23 with a crew of twenty, two-thirds the size of some other oil tanker crews. Exxon claimed that new technology enabled the smaller crew to handle the ship safely, and the Coast Guard had approved Exxon's decision to reduce the size of the crew.

Nevertheless, crew members often had to work for long stretches with little sleep, and averaged 140 hours of overtime work per month. Exhaustion was common.

For two hours the Exxon Valdez was guided out of port by a harbor pilot, who turned control of the vessel over to Captain Hazelwood and left the ship at 11 :24 p.m. At 11 :25 Captain Hazelwood radioed the Coast Guard and received permission to steer south to the in-bound shipping lane. Approximately fifteen minutes later, Captain Hazelwood turned control of the ship over to his third mate, Gregory T. Cousins, and returned to his cabin after giving Cousins directions on how to steer clear of the ice in Prince William Sound. Though prohibited by Coast Guard regulations, Hazelwood had been drinking in town within four hours of the ship's departure, and was found to be legally drunk when tested ten hours after the grounding. Third Mate Cousins did not have the license required to pilot the ship in Prince William Sound, but he was now in charge of the tanker.

The Exxon Valdez and an unloading barge after the grounding. Who should be considered responsible for the Alaskan oil spill in 1989?    ☞

　　埃克森·瓦尔迪兹号在3月23日晚上9点载着20名船员（规模是其他油轮船员数的三分之二）离开港口。埃克森号声称新技术能在船员人数减少的情况下保证安全驾驶，而海岸警卫队也批准了埃克森号缩小船员规模的决定。然而，船员们在航程中常常不得不长时间工作，只能睡很少的觉，平均每月要加班140个小时，疲劳驾船是常有的事。

　　埃克森·瓦尔迪兹号在最初两小时的时间里由领航员引导开出港口。他将船的控制权转交给黑兹尔伍德船长后，于晚上11点24分下船。11点25分，黑兹尔伍德船长用无线电联系海岸警卫队，并获批转向南驶入回程航道。大约15分钟后，黑兹尔伍德船长将船的驾驶权转交三副格里高利·T. 卡津斯，并在交待了卡津斯有关如何绕开威廉王子湾的冰山等注意事项后，回到了自己的船舱。尽管海岸警卫队明文禁止船员饮酒驾船，黑兹尔伍德仍然在开船前4小时在城里喝了不少酒，以至于在船触礁10小时后，还能测出他在法定醉酒标准之内。同时，三副卡津斯并没有在威廉王子湾领航的有效执照，但他现在却主管着整艘油轮。

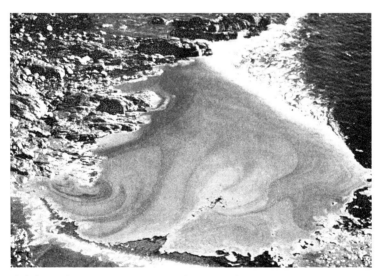

埃克森·瓦尔迪兹号和它触礁后卸货的驳船，哪个应当为1989年阿拉斯加漏油事件负责？

The passage through the Sound is so narrow that ships rely heavily on the Coast Guard when they sail that particular area. The Coast Guard, however, had lost track of the Exxon Valdez. The Guard claimed that difficult weather conditions, poor equipment, and a change of-shift prevented the watchman from following the tanker on radar.

Shortly after midnight the Exxon Valdez ran aground. Following Captain Hazelwood's instructions, Third Mate Cousins had steered the ship outside the established shipping lanes in order to avoid ice floes; he acted too late in turning back toward the channel, and the ship ran hard aground on Bligh Reef. Oil began rapidly leaking into Prince William Sound.

The damage done by the wreck of the Exxon Valdez was devastating. The harm to the fish and wildlife in the area was enormous. Beaches and shoreline were blackened and recovery would be slow. Despite previous assurances by the oil companies that operated in the area that they could control any oil spill, months and even years later the effects of the oil spill could still be seen along the Alaska coastline.

　　穿越威廉王子湾的通道很狭窄，因此在这片特殊区域过往的船只必须依靠海岸警卫队的指引。然而，海岸警卫队却与埃克森·瓦尔迪兹号失去了联系。警卫队声称，糟糕的天气、陈旧的设备以及警卫换班等因素，使海岸警卫队未能在雷达上及时追踪到这艘油轮。

　　进入午夜之后没多久，埃克森·瓦尔迪兹号搁浅了。根据黑兹尔伍德船长的指示，三副卡津斯掉转方向，让船驶离既定航道，以避开浮冰。但他没能来得及将船驶回海峡，船就重重地撞上了布莱礁。船上装载的原油迅速开始泄露到威廉王子湾中。

　　埃克森·瓦尔迪兹号的失事所造成的灾难是毁灭性的，原油泄漏对这片区域内的鱼类和野生生物造成了巨大的伤害。沙滩和海岸线都变黑了，并且恢复起来非常缓慢。尽管在这片区域内从事经营的石油公司曾事先保证他们会控制任何漏油事故，然而在几个月甚至几年后的阿拉斯加海岸沿线，仍可以看到此次漏油事故的影响。

## Using the Lesson

1. Write a letter to the editor defending the actions of one of the four individuals or groups involved in the story you have just read.

2. Do library research to find out more about the Exxon Valdez oil spill and the damage it caused. Write an analysis of the incident and explain you conclusions as to who should be held responsible.

Who should be responsible for cleaning and caring for wildlife and the environment during and after an oil spill?  ☞

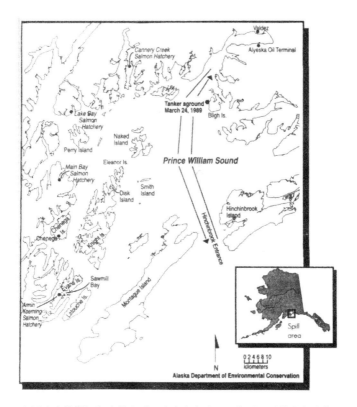

在漏油事故期间和事故之后，谁应当为清理环境以及看管野生生物负责？

## 知识运用

1. 在你刚刚读过的故事中涉及了四个人或者四组人，给编辑写一封信，为当中任何一个人或一组人的行为进行辩护。

2. 到图书馆搜索资料，寻找更多有关埃克森·瓦尔迪兹号漏油事故及其造成的灾难的信息。针对这场事故写一篇分析文章，并对谁应为此事承担责任的问题说明你的结论。

| Intellectual Tool Chart for Deciding Who Is Responsible | | | |
|---|---|---|---|
| 1. What is the event or situation in question? | | | |
| 2. Who are the persons who might be considered responsible? | | | |
| 3. How might each person be considered to have caused the event or situation? | | | |
| 4. What duty or obligation, if any, did the person's conduct violate or fail to fulfill? | | | |
| 5. What was the person's state of mind? Consider<br>a. Intent<br>b. Recklessness<br>c. Carelessness<br>d. Knowledge of probable consequences | | | |
| 6. Did the person lack control? Could he or she have acted differently? Explain your answer. | | | |
| 7. What important values, interests, or responsibilities, if any, excuse the person's conduct? | | | |

| 判定责任人的知识工具表 | | | |
|---|---|---|---|
| 1.要讨论的事件或事情是什么? | | | |
| 2.哪些人可能要对这件事负责? | | | |
| 3.当中涉及的每个人是如何导致了事件或事情的发生? | | | |
| 4.这个人的行为违背了或未能承担什么责任或义务(如果有的话)? | | | |
| 5.这个人的精神状态是什么? 请考虑: <br> a.故意 <br> b.鲁莽 <br> c.粗心 <br> d.了解可能产生的结果 | | | |
| 6.这个人是否失去了控制? 他是否可以有不同的行为方式选择? 解释你的答案。 | | | |
| 7.如果有的话,什么重要的价值观、利益或责任能为这个人的行为解释? | | | |

## LESSON 10

## Who Should Be Considered Responsible for Achieving the Peace Treaty?

---

### Purpose of Lesson

We often want to determine responsibility to punish a person or prevent the person or others from wrongdoing. There are other times, however, when we want to decide responsibility to give recognition or a reward to someone who deserves it. In this lesson you evaluate and take a position on who deserves the credit for an achievement.

When you have completed the lesson, you should be able to explain how you used the intellectual tools you have learned to decide who should be rewarded for achieving a peace treaty.

---

### Critical Thinking Exercise

**EVALUATING, TAKING, AND DEFENDING A POSITION**

Your class will conduct a meeting of an imaginary organization, the International Peace Award Committee. Each year this committee gives a prestigious award, along with a sizable grant of money, to the individuals or groups most responsible for contributing to world peace that year.

The class will be divided into small groups of three or five students to complete this exercise. Each group should read "The Peace Treaty" and then review the section "Information to Be Considered in Determining Responsibility." Next, each group should answer the "What do you think?" questions. Follow the instructions in "Preparing for and Conducting the Hearing."

# 第十课：谁应该被视为"签订和平协议"的责任人？

## 本课目标

我们要对责任进行判定，通常是为了惩罚某人，或阻止、避免某些人做错事。然而有时候，我们对责任的判定也是为了肯定或奖励那些值得受到嘉奖的人。在本课中，你们将对谁应当因某种成就而受到奖励进行评估并做决定。

完成本课学习后，针对谁应因缔结和平协议而受到嘉奖的问题，你们应当能够解释自己是如何运用学过的知识工具来判定责任人的。

## 重点思考练习

### 评估、选择和论证某种观点

你们班将为一个虚拟的组织——国际和平大奖委员会举办一次模拟会议。每年这个委员会都将为当年对世界和平做出最大贡献的个人或团体颁发这项声望卓著的大奖，同时还要向得奖人或团体颁发一笔数目可观的奖金。

要完成此次练习，全班将分成若干个3到5个人的小组。每组都要阅读下文的"和平协议"，并仔细阅读"判定责任时需要考虑的信息"这一部分。接下来每组都要回答"你怎么看？"这一部分的问题，并按照"准备并举行听证会"中的说明举行会议。

**The Peace Treaty**

The Valley of Potomus is one of the most fertile parts of the Planet Scone. Since before recorded history, the valley has been populated by people drawn by its rich resources. From earliest times to the present day, diverse groups-from small tribes to modem nations-have disputed ownership of the land.

During the past thirty years, two industrialized nations, Samia and Ganges, have dominated the area. Although constantly at war with each other, neither country is able to achieve complete victory over the other. Each nation devotes the bulk of its resources to war.

In both countries, opinion is divided over how to achieve peace. There are some in each nation who believe that peace can not be accomplished without total surrender of the other. Others believe that continued fighting is inevitable and must be endured. Some people, sickened by the continual destruction of life and property, want peace at any price. Some people believe that compromise is the key; they want to negotiate a peace that will meet the needs of both nations.

The Situation in Samia. In a recent election, the people of Samia elected Artemis, a moderate who favored a peace treaty. During the election, Artemis was opposed by a number of powerful groups, including the owners of the major newspapers and television stations. Samia's legislature is composed of representatives of five parties; none has a majority. It is clear that for a treaty to be passed by the required two-thirds vote, members of the different parties would have to cooperate.

The Situation in Ganges. Three years ago in Ganges, Porter, who like Artemis favored a negotiated peace treaty, was elected by a narrow margin over a more militant opponent. As in Samia, the legislature of Ganges is split among a number of parties; none has a controlling vote. Unlike Samia, in Ganges the news media favor a negotiated settlement of differences. However, a militant religious sect that represents a large segment of the population, opposes a peace settlement.

Since Artemis's election, representatives of both governments have met often. They are drafting a peace treaty that they hope will receive the support of the majority of each country's legislature and citizens.

### 和平协议

坡托姆斯河谷是司康行星上最肥沃的地区之一，从有历史记载之前开始，就有人类因河谷丰富的资源而定居于此。从远古时代至今，无数群体（从小部落到现代国家）都在争夺这块土地的所有权。

在过去30年里，两个工业化国家——萨尔尼亚和刚吉斯，一直统治着这一区域。尽管双方之间不断发生战争，但它们都未能取得对彼此的绝对胜利，两国都为常年战争付出了巨大的财力和物力。

两国国内也对如何实现两国之间的和平产生了分歧。各国都有一部分人相信和平是无法实现的，除非一方向另一方彻底投降；也都各自有一部分人认为持续的战争是无法避免的，除了忍受别无他法。还有一些人再也不想自己的生活和财产持续遭受破坏，愿意不惜一切代价获得和平。有人认为，和平的关键是妥协，他们希望能通过谈判签订一份能满足两国要求的和平协议。

萨尔尼亚国内：在最近的一次选举中，萨尔尼亚人选出了一位温和的、支持签订和平协议的领袖阿尔特弥斯。在选举过程中，阿尔特弥斯遭到许多势力集团（包括国内许多重要报纸和电视台所有者）的反对。萨尔尼亚的议会由五个党派的代表组成，其中没有一个党派在议会中占据绝对多数席位。很明显，要想在议会中通过和平协议的提案，就要获得法律规定的三分之二选票，不同党派的成员必须合作。

刚吉斯国内：3年前，像阿尔特弥斯一样支持通过协商达成和平协议的波特以微弱优势击败激进的竞争对手，当选刚吉斯的国家领袖。和萨尔尼亚一样，刚吉斯的议会也分裂为许多党派，都不占有多数席位。和萨尔尼亚不一样的是，刚吉斯的新闻媒体倾向通过协商解决两国的分歧，有一个代表大部分民众意见的激进宗教派别则反对和平解决争端。

自从阿尔特弥斯当选后，两国政府的代表开始频繁接触。他们起草了一份和平协议，希望得到各自国家的议会及大多数公民的支持。

The negotiation process is not an easy one and extremists in both nations are attempting to undermine the peace efforts. At the same time, supporters of the negotiations are working hard to build support for the forthcoming treaty.

Artemis's and Porter's associates have circulated drafts of the proposed treaty to key members of each nation's legislature. Artemis's staff is working to convince the opposing members of the news media to reduce their violent opposition to the treaty. Porter's associates are making similar attempts to soften the opposition in Ganges among the militants.

Finally the negotiators called a summit meeting amid great ceremony, and with worldwide news coverage, Artemis and Porter met, accompanied by the negotiators and the major dignitaries of both nations.

Although members of each group knew the treaty could not be put into effect until ratified by the legislatures of each nation, they believed that most of the necessary groundwork had been done. Two months later, after considerable effort and negotiation within each nation, the treaty was ratified. After years of struggle and the loss of thousands of lives, the nations finally achieved a peace treaty that provided a solution to the major problems that divided them.

 How can you decide who should be considered responsible for successfully negotiating a peace treaty between two hostile nations?  ☞

　　谈判的过程并不顺利。两个国家的极端主义分子都试图破坏双方缔结和平的努力。而同时，协商谈判的支持者们也竭尽全力为即将实现的和平协议提供支持。

　　阿尔特弥斯和波特的同僚们将协议草案提交给两国议会的主要成员传阅。阿尔特弥斯的幕僚致力于说服新闻媒体中的反对者减少对该和平协议的激烈反对。而波特的下属则同样尝试缓和刚吉斯激进派的反对力度。

　　最终，协议的谈判者们召开了一次两国首脑会议，举行了盛大的庆典，并向全球发布新闻报道。阿尔特弥斯与波特进行了会晤，随行的有双方的协议谈判者及两国政要。

　　尽管双方谈判组的成员都清楚，在两国议会正式批准之前，这份和平协议是无法生效的，但他们坚信自己已经完成了绝大部分的基础工作。两个月后，在双方付出极大努力，反复磋商之后，这份和平协议正式获得两国议会批准。经过连年战争，千万条生命的牺牲之后，两国终于缔结了和平协议，为导致两国分歧的主要问题提供了有效的解决方案。

如何判定谁是让两个敌对国家成功缔结和平协议的责任人？

**Information to Be Considered in Determining Responsibility**

Listed below are some principal persons and groups involved in the peace process between Samia and Ganges. Review the list and add any others that you think should be included. Then answer the "What do you think?" questions.

---

### <u>Samia</u>

Artemis

Government

Negotiators and assistants

Artemis's staff

Leaders of minority parties who convinced their members to support
  the treaty

Newspaper owners

TV station owners

Interest groups opposed to the treaty

Interest groups favoring the treaty


### <u>Ganges</u>

Porter

Government

Negotiators and assistants

Porter's staff

Leaders ofminority parties who convinced their members to support
  the treaty

Newspaper owners

TV station owners

Interest groups opposed to the treaty

Interest groups favoring the treaty

---

**判定责任时需要考虑的信息**

下面列出了一些萨尔尼亚与刚吉斯的和平进程中涉及的主要人物或群体。仔细阅读这份名单，加入任何你认为应当包括其中的个人或群体，然后回答"你怎么看？"这部分的问题。

---

### 萨尔尼亚

阿尔特弥斯

政府

谈判者及其助手

阿尔特弥斯的幕僚

说服其成员支持该协议的少数党领袖

报纸的所有者

电视台的所有者

反对该和平协议的利益团体

支持该和平协议的利益团体

### 刚吉斯

波特

政府

谈判者及其助手

波特的幕僚

说服其成员支持该协议的少数党领袖

报纸的所有者

电视台的所有者

反对该和平协议的利益团体

支持该和平协议的利益团体

**What do you think?**

1. Who should be considered responsible for achieving the peace treaty? Why?

2. To whom should an International Peace Award be presented? Why?

**Preparing for and Conducting the Hearing**

Each group should select a spokesperson and a recorder, then decide whom it considers primarily responsible for achieving the peace treaty, and prepare a presentation explaining why its nominee should receive the award.

The group assigned to represent the International Peace Committee should choose a chairperson and a recorder. The committee should prepare a list of questions and considerations to ask about each nominee.

Each group will have two to three minutes to present its nomination for the International Peace Award. The class as a whole should then analyze and discuss the nominations made by each of the groups and vote on which nominee should receive the award.

 What responsibility do citizens have for monitoring and influencing changes in public policy?    ☞

你怎么看?

1. 谁应被视为缔结和平协议的责任人?为什么?
2. 国际和平大奖应该颁发给谁?为什么?

**准备并举行听证会**

1. 每组都应选出一位发言人和一位记录者,然后小组讨论选出应为缔结和平协议负主要责任的人。准备陈述发言,解释为什么自己小组提名的人应该赢得国际和平大奖。
2. 模拟代表国际和平大奖委员会的小组应选出一位主席和一位记录者。委员会小组应准备一份提问清单,列出针对每个提名者的问题和考虑因素。
3. 每组将有2到3分钟时间介绍自己推荐的国际和平大奖提名者。然后全班应一起分析和讨论各组的提名人选,并投票选出哪位提名者将获得国际和平大奖。

在监督与影响公共政策的变更方面,公民负有什么责任?

## Using the Lesson

1.Imagine that you are a newspaper reporter covering the ceremony announcing the peace treaty between Sarnia and Ganges. Write an article based on the interview you have conducted with participants from both countries.

2.Write a short journal entry opposing the choice made by the International Peace Award Committee. Describe who you think should be considered responsible for achieving the peace treaty and explain your decision.

**知识运用**

1.  假设你是一位报社记者，正在报道萨尔尼亚与刚吉斯缔结和平协议的庆典，根据你对参与此次庆典的两国公民分别进行的采访，写一篇文章。

2.  写一篇简短的笔记，反对国际和平大奖委员会的最终决定。说明你认为谁应被视为缔结和平协议的责任人，并解释你的选择。

# 附录1:
# 词汇表

abridge RL2. To reduce in scope; to limit or curtail.

删减（《责任》第二课）：缩减范围；限制或减少。

agenda RL4. A list, outline, or plan of things to be considered or done.

议程（《责任》第四课）：需要考虑或完成的事项列表、纲要或计划。

Amish RL7. Members of the Mennonite religion that settled in the United States.

阿米什（《责任》第七课）：在美国定居的门诺派教徒（译者注：16世纪起源于荷兰的基督教新派）。

appointment RL1. A non-elective office or position

任命（《责任》第一课）：非选举产生的工作职位。

assignment RL1. An appointment to a post or duty.

分派（《责任》第一课）：指派担任某一职位或职责。

benefits RL3. Things that promote well-being; advantages.

利益（《责任》第三课）：使...得益；优势。

burden. RL3 Something oppressive or worrisome.

负担（《责任》第三课）：某些有压迫性的或让人烦恼的事情。

carelessness RL8. Inattentive or negligent behavior.

粗心（《责任》第八课）：漫不经心或粗心大意的行为。

civic principles RL1. A rule or code of conduct relating to citizenship.

公民原则（《责任》第一课）：一种与公民身份相关的行为准则或规范。

conscious choice RL1/RL2. A choice marked by thought.

有意识的选择（《责任》第一课、第二课）：经过思考的选择。

costs RL3. Losses or penalties incurred in gaining something.

损失（《责任》第三课）：在获得的同时随之而来的损失或惩罚。

compromise RL5. A settlement of differences between opposing sides in which each side gives up some of its claims and agrees to some of the demands of the other.

妥协（《责任》第五课）：解决争议双方分歧的某种方法，双方都各自放弃自己的某些主张，同意对方的某些要求。

constituent RL1. One of a group who elects another to represent them in public office.

选民（《责任》第一课）：一群人中选出一个人来代表群体内其他人担任公共职务。

contract RL1. A formal agreement, enforceable by law, between two or more persons or groups.

契约（《责任》第一课）：在两个或更多人之间、或群体之间达成的、具有法律强制执行效力的正式协议。

control or choice RL8. Authority or power to regulate or choose.

控制或选择（《责任》第八课）：管控或选择的权威、权力。

dilemma RL6. A situation involving a choice between two equally unsatisfactory alternatives.

困境（《责任》第六课）：需要在两种同样不理想的选项之间做选择的境况。

efficiency RL3. Effective operation as measured by comparing production with cost-as in energy, time, and money.

效率（《责任》第三课）：通过产品和成本之间的对比，衡量在能源、时间和金钱方面的有效运行。

ex officio RL4. Originally from Latin. To have privilege or burden by virtue of one's office or position.

依据职权（《责任》第四课）：来源于拉丁文。由于一个人的公职或职位所拥有的特权或责任。（译者注：在本书中"ex officio member"是指"当然成员"）

Fourth Amendment RL2. The right of the people to be secure in their persons, houses, papers and effects, against unreasonable searches and seizures, shall not be violated, and no Warrants shall issue, but upon probable cause, supported by Oath or affirmation, and particularly describing the place to be searched, and the persons or things to be seized.

美国联邦宪法第四修正案（《责任》第二课）：人民的人身、住宅、文件和财产不受无理搜查和扣押的权利，不得侵犯。除依照合理根据，以宣誓或代誓宣言保证，并具体说明搜查地点和扣押的人或物，不得发出搜查和扣押状。

intent RL8. Aim or purpose.

故意（《责任》第八课）：（有）目的或意图。

interest RL5. A right to or claim on something.

利益（《责任》第五课）：对某事（物）的支配权或有权要求做某事得到某物。

Hippocratic oath RL2. An oath embodying a code of medical ethics usually taken by those about to begin medical practice.

希波克拉底誓言（《责任》第二课）：通常由即将开始行医的人所宣读的一份有关医道德准则的誓言。

knowledge of probable consequences RL8. Expectations marked by reason.

了解可能产生的结果（《责任》第八课）：理性的期望。

moral principle RL1. A rule of custom or code for behavior that differentiates between right and wrong.

道德原则（《责任》第一课）：一种用来辨别是非的行为准则或习俗规则。

obligation RL1. Something one is bound to do as a duty or responsibility.

义务（《责任》第一课）：出于某种职责或责任一个人必须要做的某事。

predictable (predictability) RL3. Capable of being foretold on the basis of observation, experience, or scientific reason.

可预见的（《责任》第三课）：在观察、经验或科学理性的基础上能够被预言的。

public hearing RL4. Open session in which witnesses are heard and testimony is taken about an issue relevant to the community.

公共听证会（《责任》第四课）：听取和采纳某个与社区相关的议题的证言与证据的公开会议。

reckless (recklessness) RL8. Lacking proper caution; careless of the consequences of one's actions.

鲁莽（《责任》第八课）：缺乏适当的谨慎；不顾个人行为的后果。

relative importance RL4. Not of absolute or independent significance--comparative.

相对重要性（《责任》第四课）：不是绝对的或单独的重要性（可比较的）。

resentment RL3. A feeling of indignant displeasure or persistent ill will at something regarded as a wrong, insult, or injury.

不满（《责任》第三课）：对某些被看做是错误、侮辱或伤害的事情感到愤怒的不悦或坚定的厌恶。

resources RL5. Equipment, experience, or financial means of supply or support; natural sources of wealth or revenue.

资源（《责任》第五课）：用于供给或支持的设备、经验或财政手段；财富或收入的自然来源。

responsibility RL1. The ability to answer for one's conduct and obligations; ability to choose for oneself between right and wrong.

责任（《责任》第一课）：为某人的行为和义务负责的能力；在对错之间做出抉择的能力。

reward (individual rewards) RL3. Something given or received in return for some act, service, or attainment.

回报（《责任》第三课）：赠予或收到某物，作为某些行为、服务或成就的回馈和报酬。

security RL3. Freedom from risk or danger.

安全（《责任》第三课）：免受威胁或免于危险的自由。

state of mind RL8. A mental or emotional disposition; mood.

精神状态（《责任》第八课）：某种精神或情感状况；情绪。

summons RL2. A call by authority to appear at a place named to attend to a duty.

传唤（《责任》第二课）：权威（机构）通知（当事人）到指定地点履行某种责任。

unreasonable search and seizure RL2. Searching a suspect or taking possession of a suspect's belongings without a warrant or without fear that a crime is about to be committed.

非法搜查和扣押（《责任》第二课）：没有搜查令或无惧罪行将要发生而搜查某个嫌疑人或扣押嫌犯的财产。

urgency RL5. The condition of calling for immediate action or attention.

紧迫程度（《责任》第五课）：必须立刻采取行动或予以关注的状况。

value RL5. A principle, standard, or quality considered worthwhile or desirable.

价值观（《责任》第五课）：被认为是有价值的或理想的准则、标准或品质。

warranty RL2. A written guarantee of the integrity of a product and of the maker's responsibility for the repair or replacement of defective parts.

保证（《责任》第二课）：有关某一产品的完整性、以及制造商负责维修与更换不良零件的书面担保。

## 附录2：

### The Constitution of the United States

We the People of the United States, in<sup>注</sup> Order to form a more perfect Union, establish Justice, insure domestic Tranquility, provide for the common defence, promote the general Welfare, and secure the Blessings of Liberty to ourselves and our Posterity, do ordain and establish this Constitution for the United States of America.

### Article. I.

**Section. 1**    All legislative Powers herein granted shall be vested in a Congress of the United States, which shall consist of a Senate and House of Representatives.

**Section. 2**    The House of Representatives shall be composed of Members chosen every second Year by the People of the several States, and the Electors in each State shall have the Qualifications requisite for Electors of the most numerous Branch of the State Legislature.

No Person shall be a Representative who shall not have attained to the Age of twenty five Years, and been seven Years a Citizen of the United States, and who shall not, when elected, be an Inhabitant of that State in which he shall be chosen.

Representatives and direct Taxes shall be apportioned among the several States which may be included within this Union, according to their respective Numbers, which shall be determined by adding to the whole Number of free Persons, including those bound to Service for a Term of Years, and excluding Indians not taxed, three fifths of all other Persons. The actual Enumeration shall be made within three Years after the first Meeting of the Congress of the United States, and within every subsequent Term of ten Years, in such Manner as they shall by Law direct. The Number of Representatives shall not exceed one for every thirty Thousand, but each State shall have at Least one Representative; and until

---

注：原文：美国国家档案馆

　　http://www.archives.gov/exhibits/charters/constitution_transcript.html

## 美利坚合众国宪法

我们合众国人民，为建立更完善的联邦，树立正义，保障国内安宁，提供共同防务，促进公共福利，并使我们自己和后代得享自由的幸福，特为美利坚合众国制定本宪法。

### 第一条

第一款　本宪法授予的全部立法权，属于由参议院和众议院组成的合众国国会。

第二款　众议院由各州人民每两年选举产生的众议员组成。每个州的选举人须具备该州州议会人数最多一院选举人所必需的资格。

凡年龄不满二十五岁，成为合众国公民不满七年，在一州当选时不是该州居民者，不得担任众议员。

〔众议员名额和直接税税额，在本联邦可包括的各州中，按照各自人口比例进行分配。各州人口数，按自由人总数加上所有其他人口的五分之三予以确定。自由人总数包括必须服一定年限劳役的人，但不包括未被征税的印第安人。〕① 人口的实际统计在合众国国会第一次会议后三年内和此后每十年内，依法律规定的方式进行。每三万人选出的众议员人数不得超过一名，但每州至少须有一名众议员；在进行上述人口统计以前，新罕布什尔州有权选出三名，马萨诸塞州八名，罗得岛州和普罗维登斯种植地一名，康涅狄格州五名，纽约州六名，新泽西州四名，宾夕法尼亚州八名，特拉华州一名，马里兰州六名，弗吉尼亚州十名，北卡罗来纳州五名，南卡罗来纳州五名，佐治亚州三名。

such enumeration shall be made, the State of New Hampshire shall be entitled to chuse three, Massachusetts eight, Rhode-Island and Providence Plantations one, Connecticut five, New-York six, New Jersey four, Pennsylvania eight, Delaware one, Maryland six, Virginia ten, North Carolina five, South Carolina five, and Georgia three.

When vacancies happen in the Representation from any State, the Executive Authority thereof shall issue Writs of Election to fill such Vacancies.

The House of Representatives shall chuse their Speaker and other Officers; and shall have the sole Power of Impeachment.

**Section. 3**    The Senate of the United States shall be composed of two Senators from each State, chosen by the Legislature thereof for six Years; and each Senator shall have one Vote.

Immediately after they shall be assembled in Consequence of the first Election, they shall be divided as equally as may be into three Classes. The Seats of the Senators of the first Class shall be vacated at the Expiration of the second Year, of the second Class at the Expiration of the fourth Year, and of the third Class at the Expiration of the sixth Year, so that one third may be chosen every second Year; and if Vacancies happen by Resignation, or otherwise, during the Recess of the Legislature of any State, the Executive thereof may make temporary Appointments until the next Meeting of the Legislature, which shall then fill such Vacancies.

No Person shall be a Senator who shall not have attained to the Age of thirty Years, and been nine Years a Citizen of the United States, and who shall not, when elected, be an Inhabitant of that State for which he shall be chosen.

The Vice President of the United States shall be President of the Senate, but shall have no Vote, unless they be equally divided.

The Senate shall chuse their other Officers, and also a President pro tempore, in the Absence of the Vice President, or when he shall exercise the Office of President of the United States.

The Senate shall have the sole Power to try all Impeachments. When sitting for that Purpose, they shall be on Oath or Affirmation. When the President of the United States is tried, the Chief Justice shall preside: And no Person shall be convicted without the Concurrence of two thirds of the Members present.

任何一州代表出现缺额时，该州行政当局应发布选举令，以填补此项缺额。

众议院选举本院议长和其他官员，并独自拥有弹劾权。

第三款　合众国参议院由［每州州议会选举的］②两名参议员组成，任期六年；每名参议员有一票表决权。

参议员在第一次选举后集会时，立即分为人数尽可能相等的三个组。第一组参议员席位在第二年年终空出，第二组参议员席位在第四年年终空出，第三组参议员席位在第六年年终空出，以便三分之一的参议员得每二年改选一次。［在任何一州州议会休会期间，如因辞职或其他原因而出现缺额时，该州行政长官在州议会下次集会填补此项缺额前，得任命临时参议员。］③

凡年龄不满三十岁，成为合众国公民不满九年，在一州当选时不是该州居民者，不得担任参议员。

合众国副总统任参议院议长，但除非参议员投票时赞成票和反对票相等，无表决权。

参议院选举本院其他官员，并在副总统缺席或行使合众国总统职权时，选举一名临时议长。

参议院独自拥有审判一切弹劾案的权力。为此目的而开庭时，全体参议员须宣誓或作代誓宣言。合众国总统受审时，最高法院首席大法官主持审判。无论何人，非经出席参议员三分之二的同意，不得被定罪。

Judgment in Cases of Impeachment shall not extend further than to removal from Office, and disqualification to hold and enjoy any Office of honor, Trust or Profit under the United States: but the Party convicted shall nevertheless be liable and subject to Indictment, Trial, Judgment and Punishment, according to Law.

**Section. 4**    The Times, Places and Manner of holding Elections for Senators and Representatives, shall be prescribed in each State by the Legislature thereof; but the Congress may at any time by Law make or alter such Regulations, except as to the Places of chusing Senators.

The Congress shall assemble at least once in every Year, and such Meeting shall be on the first Monday in December, unless they shall by Law appoint a different Day.

**Section. 5**    Each House shall be the Judge of the Elections, Returns and Qualifications of its own Members, and a Majority of each shall constitute a Quorum to do Business; but a smaller Number may adjourn from day to day, and may be authorized to compel the Attendance of absent Members, in such Manner, and under such Penalties as each House may provide.

Each House may determine the Rules of its Proceedings, punish its Members for disorderly Behaviour, and, with the Concurrence of two thirds, expel a Member.

Each House shall keep a Journal of its Proceedings, and from time to time publish the same, excepting such Parts as may in their Judgment require Secrecy; and the Yeas and Nays of the Members of either House on any question shall, at the Desire of one fifth of those Present, be entered on the Journal.

Neither House, during the Session of Congress, shall, without the Consent of the other, adjourn for more than three days, nor to any other Place than that in which the two Houses shall be sitting.

**Section. 6**    The Senators and Representatives shall receive a Compensation for their Services, to be ascertained by Law, and paid out of the Treasury of the United States. They shall in all Cases, except Treason, Felony and Breach of the Peace, be privileged from Arrest during their Attendance at the Session of their respective Houses, and in going to and returning from the same; and for any Speech or Debate in either House, they shall not be questioned in any other Place.

弹劾案的判决，不得超出免职和剥夺担任和享有合众国属下有荣誉、有责任或有薪金的任何职务的资格。但被定罪的人，仍可依法起诉、审判、判决和惩罚。

第四款　举行参议员和众议员选举的时间、地点和方式，在每个州由该州议会规定。但除选举参议员的地点外，国会得随时以法律制定或改变这类规定。

国会每年至少开会一次，除非国会以法律另订日期外，此会议在［十二月第一个星期一］④举行。

第五款　每院是本院议员的选举、选举结果报告和资格的裁判者。每院议员过半数，即构成议事的法定人数；但不足法定人数时，得逐日休会，并有权按每院规定的方式和罚则，强迫缺席议员出席会议。

每院得规定本院议事规则，惩罚本院议员扰乱秩序的行为，并经三之二议员的同意开除议员。

每院应有本院会议记录，并不时予以公布，但它认为需要保密的部分除外。每院议员对于任何问题的赞成票和反对票，在出席议员五分之一的请求下，应载入会议记录。

在国会开会期间，任何一院，未经另一院同意，不得休会三日以上，也不得到非两院开会的任何地方休会。

第六款　参议员和众议员应得到服务的报酬，此项报酬由法律确定并由合众国国库支付。他们除犯叛国罪、重罪和妨害治安罪外，在一切情况下都享有在出席各自议院会议期间和往返于各自议院途中不受逮捕的特权。他们不得因在各自议院发表的演说或辩论而在任何其他地方受到质问。

No Senator or Representative shall, during the Time for which he was elected, be appointed to any civil Office under the Authority of the United States, which shall have been created, or the Emoluments whereof shall have been encreased during such time; and no Person holding any Office under the United States, shall be a Member of either House during his Continuance in Office.

**Section. 7**    All Bills for raising Revenue shall originate in the House of Representatives; but the Senate may propose or concur with Amendments as on other Bills.

Every Bill which shall have passed the House of Representatives and the Senate, shall, before it become a Law, be presented to the President of the United States: If he approve he shall sign it, but if not he shall return it, with his Objections to that House in which it shall have originated, who shall enter the Objections at large on their Journal, and proceed to reconsider it. If after such Reconsideration two thirds of that House shall agree to pass the Bill, it shall be sent, together with the Objections, to the other House, by which it shall likewise be reconsidered, and if approved by two thirds of that House, it shall become a Law. But in all such Cases the Votes of both Houses shall be determined by yeas and Nays, and the Names of the Persons voting for and against the Bill shall be entered on the Journal of each House respectively. If any Bill shall not be returned by the President within ten Days (Sundays excepted) after it shall have been presented to him, the Same shall be a Law, in like Manner as if he had signed it, unless the Congress by their Adjournment prevent its Return, in which Case it shall not be a Law.

Every Order, Resolution, or Vote to which the Concurrence of the Senate and House of Representatives may be necessary (except on a question of Adjournment) shall be presented to the President of the United States; and before the Same shall take Effect, shall be approved by him, or being disapproved by him, shall be repassed by two thirds of the Senate and House of Representatives, according to the Rules and Limitations prescribed in the Case of a Bill.

**Section. 8**    The Congress shall have Power To lay and collect Taxes, Duties, Imposts and Excises, to pay the Debts and provide for the common Defence and general Welfare of the United States; but all Duties, Imposts and Excises shall be uniform throughout the United States;

参议员或众议员在当选任期内，不得被任命担任在此期间设置或增薪的合众国管辖下的任何文官职务。凡在合众国属下任职者，在继续任职期间不得担任任何一院议员。

第七款　所有征税议案应首先在众议院提出，但参议院得像对其他议案一样，提出或同意修正案。

众议院和参议院通过的每一议案，在成为法律前须送交合众国总统。总统如批准该议案，即应签署；如不批准，则应将该议案同其反对意见退回最初提出该议案的议院。该院应特此项反对见详细载入本院会议记录并进行复议。如经复议后，该院三分之二议员同意通过该议案，该议案连同反对意见应一起送交另一议院，并同样由该院进行复议，如经该院三分之二议员赞同，该议案即成为法律。但在所有这类情况下，两院表决都由赞成票和反对票决定；对该议案投赞成票和反对票的议员姓名应分别载入每一议院会议记录。如任何议案在送交总统后十天内（星期日除外）未经总统退回，该议案如同总统已签署一样，即成为法律，除非因国会休会而使该议案不能退回，在此种情况下，该议案不能成为法律。

凡须由参议院和众议院一致同意的每项命令、决议或表决（关于休会问题除外），须送交合众国总统，该项命令、决议或表决在生效前，须由总统批准，如总统不批准，则按照关于议案所规定的规则和限制，由参议院和众议院三分之二议员重新通过。

第八款　国会有权：

规定和征收直接税、进口税、捐税和其他税，以偿付国债、提供合众国共同防务和公共福利，但一切进口税、捐税和其他税应全国统一；

To borrow Money on the credit of the United States;

To regulate Commerce with foreign Nations, and among the several States, and with the Indian Tribes;

To establish an uniform Rule of Naturalization, and uniform Laws on the subject of Bankruptcies throughout the United States;

To coin Money, regulate the Value thereof, and of foreign Coin, and fix the Standard of Weights and Measures;

To provide for the Punishment of counterfeiting the Securities and current Coin of the United States;

To establish Post Offices and post Roads;

To promote the Progress of Science and useful Arts, by securing for limited Times to Authors and Inventors the exclusive Right to their respective Writings and Discoveries;

To constitute Tribunals inferior to the supreme Court;

To define and punish Piracies and Felonies committed on the high Seas, and Offences against the Law of Nations;

To declare War, grant Letters of Marque and Reprisal, and make Rules concerning Captures on Land and Water;

To raise and support Armies, but no Appropriation of Money to that Use shall be for a longer Term than two Years;

To provide and maintain a Navy;

To make Rules for the Government and Regulation of the land and naval Forces;

To provide for calling forth the Militia to execute the Laws of the Union, suppress Insurrections and repel Invasions;

To provide for organizing, arming, and disciplining, the Militia, and for governing such Part of them as may be employed in the Service of the United States, reserving to the States respectively, the Appointment of the Officers, and the Authority of training the Militia according to the discipline prescribed by Congress;

以合众国的信用借款；

管制同外国的、各州之间的和同印第安部落的商业；

制定合众国全国统一的归化条例和破产法；

铸造货币，厘定本国货币和外国货币的价值，并确定度量衡的标准；

规定有关伪造合众国证券和通用货币的罚则；

设立邮政局和修建邮政道路；

保障著作家和发明家对各自著作和发明在限定期限内的专有权利，以促进科学和工艺的进步；

设立低于最高法院的法院；

界定和惩罚在公海上所犯的海盗罪和重罪以及违反国际法的犯罪行为；

宣战，颁发掳获敌船许可状，制定关于陆上和水上捕获的条例；

招募陆军和供给军需，但此项用途的拨款期限不得超过两年；

建立和维持一支海军；

制定治理和管理陆海军的条例；

规定征召民兵，以执行联邦法律、镇压叛乱和击退入侵；

规定民兵的组织、装备和训练，规定用来为合众国服役的那些民兵的管理，但民兵军官的任命和按国会规定的条例训练民兵的权力，由各州保留。

To exercise exclusive Legislation in all Cases whatsoever, over such District (not exceeding ten Miles square) as may, by Cession of particular States, and the Acceptance of Congress, become the Seat of the Government of the United States, and to exercise like Authority over all Places purchased by the Consent of the Legislature of the State in which the Same shall be, for the Erection of Forts, Magazines, Arsenals, dock-Yards, and other needful Buildings;--And To make all Laws which shall be necessary and proper for carrying into Execution the foregoing Powers, and all other Powers vested by this Constitution in the Government of the United States, or in any Department or Officer thereof.

**Section. 9**    The Migration or Importation of such Persons as any of the States now existing shall think proper to admit, shall not be prohibited by the Congress prior to the Year one thousand eight hundred and eight, but a Tax or duty may be imposed on such Importation, not exceeding ten dollars for each Person.

The Privilege of the Writ of Habeas Corpus shall not be suspended, unless when in Cases of Rebellion or Invasion the public Safety may require it.

No Bill of Attainder or ex post facto Law shall be passed.

No Capitation, or other direct, Tax shall be laid, unless in Proportion to the Census or enumeration herein before directed to be taken.

No Tax or Duty shall be laid on Articles exported from any State.

No Preference shall be given by any Regulation of Commerce or Revenue to the Ports of one State over those of another; nor shall Vessels bound to, or from, one State, be obliged to enter, clear, or pay Duties in another.

No Money shall be drawn from the Treasury, but in Consequence of Appropriations made by Law; and a regular Statement and Account of the Receipts and Expenditures of all public Money shall be published from time to time.

No Title of Nobility shall be granted by the United States: And no Person holding any Office of Profit or Trust under them, shall, without the Consent of the Congress, accept of any present, Emolument, Office, or Title, of any kind whatever, from any King, Prince, or foreign State.

对于由某些州让与合众国、经国会接受而成为合众国政府所在地的地区（不得超过十平方英里），在任何情况下都行使独有的立法权；对于经州议会同意、由合众国在该州购买的用于建造要塞、弹药库、兵工厂、船坞和其他必要建筑物的一切地方，行使同样的权力；以及制定为行使上述各项权力和由本宪法授予合众国政府或其任何部门或官员的一切其他权力所必要和适当的所有法律。

第九款　现有任何一州认为得准予入境之人的迁移或入境，在一千八百零八年以前，国会不得加以禁止，但对此种人的入境，每人可征不超过十美元的税。不得中止人身保护状的特权，除非发生叛乱或入侵时公共安全要求中止这项特权。

不得通过公民权利剥夺法案或追溯既往的法律。

［除依本宪法上文规定的人口普查或统计的比例，不得征收人头税或其他直接税。］⑤

对于从任何一州输出的货物，不得征税。

任何商业或税收条例，都不得给予一州港口以优惠于他州港口的待遇；开往或开出一州的船舶，不得被强迫在他州入港、出港或纳税。

除根据法律规定的拨款外，不得从国库提取款项。一切公款收支的定期报告书和账目，应不时予以公布。

合众国不得授予贵族爵位。凡在合众国属下担任任何有薪金或有责任的职务的人，未经国会同意，不得从任何国王、君主或外国接受任何礼物、俸禄、官职或任何一种爵位。

**Section. 10**    No State shall enter into any Treaty, Alliance, or Confederation; grant Letters of Marque and Reprisal; coin Money; emit Bills of Credit; make any Thing but gold and silver Coin a Tender in Payment of Debts; pass any Bill of Attainder, ex post facto Law, or Law impairing the Obligation of Contracts, or grant any Title of Nobility.

No State shall, without the Consent of the Congress, lay any Imposts or Duties on Imports or Exports, except what may be absolutely necessary for executing it's inspection Laws: and the net Produce of all Duties and Imposts, laid by any State on Imports or Exports, shall be for the Use of the Treasury of the United States; and all such Laws shall be subject to the Revision and Controul of the Congress.

No State shall, without the Consent of Congress, lay any Duty of Tonnage, keep Troops, or Ships of War in time of Peace, enter into any Agreement or Compact with another State, or with a foreign Power, or engage in War, unless actually invaded, or in such imminent Danger as will not admit of delay.

**Article. II.**

**Section. 1**    The executive Power shall be vested in a President of the United States of America. He shall hold his Office during the Term of four Years, and, together with the Vice President, chosen for the same Term, be elected, as follows:

Each State shall appoint, in such Manner as the Legislature thereof may direct, a Number of Electors, equal to the whole Number of Senators and Representatives to which the State may be entitled in the Congress: but no Senator or Representative, or Person holding an Office of Trust or Profit under the United States, shall be appointed an Elector.

The Electors shall meet in their respective States, and vote by Ballot for two Persons, of whom one at least shall not be an Inhabitant of the same State with themselves. And they shall make a List of all the Persons voted for, and of the Number of Votes for each; which List they shall sign and certify, and transmit sealed to the Seat of the Government of the United States, directed to the President of the Senate. The President of the Senate shall, in the Presence of the Senate and House of Representatives, open all the Certificates, and the Votes shall then be counted. The Person

第十款　任何一州都不得：缔结任何条约，参加任何同盟或邦联；颁发捕获敌船许可状；铸造货币；发行纸币；使用金银币以外的任何物品作为偿还债务的货币；通过任何公民权利剥夺法案、追溯既往的法律或损害契约义务的法律；或授予任何贵族爵位。

任何一州，未经国会同意，不得对进口货或出口货征收任何税款，但为执行本州检查法所绝对必需者除外。任何一州对进口货或出口货所征全部税款的纯收益供合众国国库使用；所有这类法律得由国会加以修正和控制。

任何一州，未经国会同意，不得征收任何船舶吨位税，不得在和平时期保持军队或战舰，不得与他州或外国缔结协定或盟约，除非实际遭到入侵或遇刻不容缓的紧迫危险时不得进行战争。

## 第二条

第一款　行政权属于美利坚合众国总统。总统任期四年，副总统的任期相同。总统和副总统按以下方法选举：每个州依照该州议会所定方式选派选举人若干人，其数目同该州在国会应有的参议员和众议员总人数相等。但参议员或众议员，或在合众国属下担任有责任或有薪金职务的人，不得被选派为选举人。

〔选举人在各自州内集会，投票选举两人，其中至少有一人不是选举人本州的居民。选举人须开列名单，写明所有被选人和每人所得票数；在该名单上签名作证，将封印后的名单送合众国政府所在地，交参议院议长收。参议院议长在参议院和众议院全体议员面前开拆所有证明书，然后计算票数。得票最多的人，如所得票数超过所选派选举人总数的半数，即为总统。如获得此种过半数票的人不止一人，且得票相等，众议院应立即投票选举其中一人为总统。如无人获得过半数票；该院应以同样方式从名单上得票最多的五人中选举一人为总统。但选举总统时，以州为单位计票，每州代表有一票表决权；三分之二的州各有一名或多名众议员出席，即构成选举总统的法定人数，选出总统需要所有州的过半数票。

having the greatest Number of Votes shall be the President, if such Number be a Majority of the whole Number of Electors appointed; and if there be more than one who have such Majority, and have an equal Number of Votes, then the House of Representatives shall immediately chuse by Ballot one of them for President; and if no Person have a Majority, then from the five highest on the List the said House shall in like Manner chuse the President. But in chusing the President, the Votes shall be taken by States, the Representation from each State having one Vote; A quorum for this purpose shall consist of a Member or Members from two thirds of the States, and a Majority of all the States shall be necessary to a Choice. In every Case, after the Choice of the President, the Person having the greatest Number of Votes of the Electors shall be the Vice President. But if there should remain two or more who have equal Votes, the Senate shall chuse from them by Ballot the Vice President.

The Congress may determine the Time of chusing the Electors, and the Day on which they shall give their Votes; which Day shall be the same throughout the United States.

No Person except a natural born Citizen, or a Citizen of the United States, at the time of the Adoption of this Constitution, shall be eligible to the Office of President; neither shall any Person be eligible to that Office who shall not have attained to the Age of thirty five Years, and been fourteen Years a Resident within the United States.

In Case of the Removal of the President from Office, or of his Death, Resignation, or Inability to discharge the Powers and Duties of the said Office, the Same shall devolve on the Vice President, and the Congress may by Law provide for the Case of Removal, Death, Resignation or Inability, both of the President and Vice President, declaring what Officer shall then act as President, and such Officer shall act accordingly, until the Disability be removed, or a President shall be elected.

The President shall, at stated Times, receive for his Services, a Compensation, which shall neither be increased nor diminished during the Period for which he shall have been elected, and he shall not receive within that Period any other Emolument from the United States, or any of them.

在每种情况下，总统选出后，得选举人票最多的人，即为副总统。但如果有两人或两人以上得票相等，参议院应投票选举其中一人为副总统。][6]

国会得确定选出选举人的时间和选举人投票日期，该日期在全合众国应为同一天。

无论何人，除生为合众国公民或在本宪法采用时已是合众国公民者外，不得当选为总统；凡年龄不满三十五岁、在合众国境内居住不满十四年者，也不得当选为总统。

[ 如遇总统被免职、死亡、辞职或丧失履行总统权力和责任的能力时，总统职务应移交副总统。国会得以法律规定在总统和副总统两人被免职、死亡、辞职或丧失任职能力时，宣布应代理总统的官员。该官员应代理总统直到总统恢复任职能力或新总统选出为止。][7]

总统在规定的时间，应得到服务报酬，此项报酬在其当选担任总统任期内不得增加或减少。总统在任期内不得接受合众国或任何一州的任何其他俸禄。

Before he enter on the Execution of his Office, he shall take the following Oath or Affirmation:--"I do solemnly swear (or affirm) that I will faithfully execute the Office of President of the United States, and will to the best of my Ability, preserve, protect and defend the Constitution of the United States."

**Section. 2**    The President shall be Commander in Chief of the Army and Navy of the United States, and of the Militia of the several States, when called into the actual Service of the United States; he may require the Opinion, in writing, of the principal Officer in each of the executive Departments, upon any Subject relating to the Duties of their respective Offices, and he shall have Power to grant Reprieves and Pardons for Offences against the United States, except in Cases of Impeachment.

He shall have Power, by and with the Advice and Consent of the Senate, to make Treaties, provided two thirds of the Senators present concur; and he shall nominate, and by and with the Advice and Consent of the Senate, shall appoint Ambassadors, other public Ministers and Consuls, Judges of the supreme Court, and all other Officers of the United States, whose Appointments are not herein otherwise provided for, and which shall be established by Law: but the Congress may by Law vest the Appointment of such inferior Officers, as they think proper, in the President alone, in the Courts of Law, or in the Heads of Departments.

The President shall have Power to fill up all Vacancies that may happen during the Recess of the Senate, by granting Commissions which shall expire at the End of their next Session.

**Section. 3**    He shall from time to time give to the Congress Information of the State of the Union, and recommend to their Consideration such Measures as he shall judge necessary and expedient; he may, on extraordinary Occasions, convene both Houses, or either of them, and in Case of Disagreement between them, with Respect to the Time of Adjournment, he may adjourn them to such Time as he shall think proper; he shall receive Ambassadors and other public Ministers; he shall take Care that the Laws be faithfully executed, and shall Commission all the Officers of the United States.

**Section. 4**    The President, Vice President and all civil Officers of the United States, shall be removed from Office on Impeachment for, and Conviction of, Treason, Bribery, or other high Crimes and Misdemeanors.

总统在开始执行职务前，应作如下宣誓或代誓宣言："我庄严宣誓（或宣言）我一定忠实执行合众国总统职务，竭尽全力维护、保护和捍卫合众国宪法"。

第二款　总统是合众国陆军、海军和征调为合众国服役的各州民兵的总司令。他得要求每个行政部门长官就他们各自职责有关的任何事项提出书面意见。他有权对危害合众国的犯罪行为发布缓刑令和赦免令，但弹劾案除外。

总统经咨询参议院和取得其同意有权缔结条约，但须经出席参议员三分之二的批准。他提名，并经咨询参议院和取得其同意，任命大使、公使和领事、最高法院法官和任命手续未由本宪法另行规定而应由法律规定的合众国所有其他官员。但国会认为适当时，得以法律将这类低级官员的任命权授予总统一人、法院或各部部长。

总统有权委任人员填补在参议院休会期间可能出现的官员缺额，此项委任在参议院下期会议结束时满期。

第三款　总统应不时向国会报告联邦情况，并向国会提出他认为必要和妥善的措施供国会审议。在非常情况下，他得召集两院或任何一院开会。如遇两院对休会时间有意见分歧时，他可使两院休会到他认为适当的时间。他应接见大使和公使。他应负责使法律切实执行，并委任合众国的所有官员。

第四款　总统、副总统和合众国的所有文职官员，因叛国、贿赂或其他重罪和轻罪而受弹劾并被定罪时，应予免职。

## Article III.

**Section. 1**   The judicial Power of the United States shall be vested in one supreme Court, and in such inferior Courts as the Congress may from time to time ordain and establish. The Judges, both of the supreme and inferior Courts, shall hold their Offices during good Behaviour, and shall, at stated Times, receive for their Services a Compensation, which shall not be diminished during their Continuance in Office.

**Section. 2**   The judicial Power shall extend to all Cases, in Law and Equity, arising under this Constitution, the Laws of the United States, and Treaties made, or which shall be made, under their Authority;--to all Cases affecting Ambassadors, other public Ministers and Consuls;--to all Cases of admiralty and maritime Jurisdiction;--to Controversies to which the United States shall be a Party;--to Controversies between two or more States;-- between a State and Citizens of another State,--between Citizens of different States,--between Citizens of the same State claiming Lands under Grants of different States, and between a State, or the Citizens thereof, and foreign States, Citizens or Subjects.

In all Cases affecting Ambassadors, other public Ministers and Consuls, and those in which a State shall be Party, the supreme Court shall have original Jurisdiction. In all the other Cases before mentioned, the supreme Court shall have appellate Jurisdiction, both as to Law and Fact, with such Exceptions, and under such Regulations as the Congress shall make.

The Trial of all Crimes, except in Cases of Impeachment, shall be by Jury; and such Trial shall be held in the State where the said Crimes shall have been committed; but when not committed within any State, the Trial shall be at such Place or Places as the Congress may by Law have directed.

**Section. 3**   Treason against the United States, shall consist only in levying War against them, or in adhering to their Enemies, giving them Aid and Comfort. No Person shall be convicted of Treason unless on the Testimony of two Witnesses to the same overt Act, or on Confession in open Court.

The Congress shall have Power to declare the Punishment of Treason, but no Attainder of Treason shall work Corruption of Blood, or Forfeiture except during the Life of the Person attainted.

## 第三条

第一款　合众国的司法权，属于最高法院和国会不时规定和设立的下级法院。最高法院和下级法院的法官如行为端正，得继续任职，并应在规定的时间得到服务报酬，此项报酬在他们继续任职期间不得减少。

第二款　司法权的适用范围包括：由于本宪法、合众国法律和根据合众国权力已缔结或将缔结的条约而产生的一切普通法的和衡平法的案件；涉及大使、公使和领事的一切案件；关于海事法和海事管辖权的一切案件；合众国为一方当事人的诉讼；两个或两个以上州之间的诉讼；〔一州和他州公民之间的诉讼；〕⑧不同州公民之间的诉讼；同州公民之间对不同州让与土地的所有权的诉讼；一州或其公民同外国或外国公民或国民之间的诉讼。

涉及大使、公使和领事以及一州为一方当事人的一切案件，最高法院具有第一审管辖权。对上述所有其他案件，不论法律方面还是事实方面，最高法院具有上诉审管辖权，但须依照国会所规定的例外和规章。

除弹劾案外，一切犯罪由陪审团审判；此种审判应在犯罪发生的州内举行；但如犯罪不发生在任何一州之内，审判应在国会以法律规定的一个或几个地点举行。

第三款　对合众国的叛国罪只限于同合众国作战，或依附其敌人，给予其敌人以帮助和鼓励。无论何人，除根据两个证人对同一明显行为的作证或本人在公开法庭上的供认，不得被定为叛国罪。

国会有权宣告对叛国罪的惩罚，但因叛国罪而剥夺公民权，不得造成血统玷污，除非在被剥夺者在世期间，也不得没收其财产。

**Article. IV.**

**Section. 1**    Full Faith and Credit shall be given in each State to the public Acts, Records, and judicial Proceedings of every other State. And the Congress may by general Laws prescribe the Manner in which such Acts, Records and Proceedings shall be proved, and the Effect thereof.

**Section. 2**    The Citizens of each State shall be entitled to all Privileges · and Immunities of Citizens in the several States.

A Person charged in any State with Treason, Felony, or other Crime, who shall flee from Justice, and be found in another State, shall on Demand of the executive Authority of the State from which he fled, be delivered up, to be removed to the State having Jurisdiction of the Crime.

No Person held to Service or Labour in one State, under the Laws thereof, escaping into another, shall, in Consequence of any Law or Regulation therein, be discharged from such Service or Labour, but shall be delivered up on Claim of the Party to whom such Service or Labour may be due.

**Section. 3**    New States may be admitted by the Congress into this Union; but no new State shall be formed or erected within the Jurisdiction of any other State; nor any State be formed by the Junction of two or more States, or Parts of States, without the Consent of the Legislatures of the States concerned as well as of the Congress.

The Congress shall have Power to dispose of and make all needful Rules and Regulations respecting the Territory or other Property belonging to the United States; and nothing in this Constitution shall be so construed as to Prejudice any Claims of the United States, or of any particular State.

**Section. 4**    The United States shall guarantee to every State in this Union a Republican Form of Government, and shall protect each of them against Invasion; and on Application of the Legislature, or of the Executive (when the Legislature cannot be convened), against domestic Violence.

## 第四条

**第一款** 每个州对于他州的公共法律、案卷和司法程序，应给予充分信任和尊重。国会得以一般法律规定这类法律、案卷和司法程序如何证明和具有的效力。

**第二款** 每个州的公民享有各州公民的一切特权和豁免权。

在任何一州被控告犯有叛国罪、重罪或其他罪行的人，逃脱法网而在他州被寻获时，应根据他所逃出之州行政当局的要求将他交出，以便解送到对犯罪行为有管辖权的州。

［根据一州法律须在该州服劳役或劳动的人，如逃往他州，不得因他州的法律或规章而免除此种劳役或劳动，而应根据有权得到此劳役或劳动之当事人的要求将他交出。］⑨

**第三款** 新州得由国会接纳加入本联邦；但不得在任何其他州的管辖范围内组成或建立新州；未经有关州议会和国会的同意，也不得合并两个或两个以上的州或几个州的一部分组成新州。

国会对于属于合众国的领土或其他财产，有权处置和制定一切必要的条例和规章。对本宪法条文不得作有损于合众国或任何一州的任何权利的解释。

**第四款** 合众国保证本联邦各州实行共和政体，保护每州免遭入侵，并应州议会或州行政长官（在州议会不能召开时）的请求平定内乱。

## Article. V.

The Congress, whenever two thirds of both Houses shall deem it necessary, shall propose Amendments to this Constitution, or, on the Application of the Legislatures of two thirds of the several States, shall call a Convention for proposing Amendments, which, in either Case, shall be valid to all Intents and Purposes, as Part of this Constitution, when ratified by the Legislatures of three fourths of the several States, or by Conventions in three fourths thereof, as the one or the other Mode of Ratification may be proposed by the Congress; Provided that no Amendment which may be made prior to the Year One thousand eight hundred and eight shall in any Manner affect the first and fourth Clauses in the Ninth Section of the first Article; and that no State, without its Consent, shall be deprived of its equal Suffrage in the Senate.

## Article. VI.

All Debts contracted and Engagements entered into, before the Adoption of this Constitution, shall be as valid against the United States under this Constitution, as under the Confederation.

This Constitution, and the Laws of the United States which shall be made in Pursuance thereof; and all Treaties made, or which shall be made, under the Authority of the United States, shall be the supreme Law of the Land; and the Judges in every State shall be bound thereby, any Thing in the Constitution or Laws of any State to the Contrary notwithstanding.

The Senators and Representatives before mentioned, and the Members of the several State Legislatures, and all executive and judicial Officers, both of the United States and of the several States, shall be bound by Oath or Affirmation, to support this Constitution; but no religious Test shall ever be required as a Qualification to any Office or public Trust under the United States.

## Article. VII.

The Ratification of the Conventions of nine States, shall be sufficient for the Establishment of this Constitution between the States so ratifying the Same.

### 第五条

国会在两院三分之二议员认为必要时，应提出本宪法的修正案，或根据各州三分之二州议会的请求，召开制宪会议提出修正案。不论哪种方式提出的修正案，经各州四分之三州议会或四分之三州制宪会议的批准，即实际成为本宪法的一部分而发生效力；采用哪种批准方式，得由国会提出建议。但［在一千八百零八年以前制定的修正案，不得以任何形式影响本宪法第一条第九款第一项和第四项］；⑩任何一州，不经其同意，不得被剥夺它在参议院的平等投票权。

### 第六条

本宪法采用前订立的一切债务和承担的一切义务，对于实行本宪法的合众国同邦联时期一样有效。

本宪法和依本宪法所制定的合众国法律，以及根据合众国的权力已缔结或将缔结的一切条约，都是全国的最高法律；每个州的法官都应受其约束，即使州的宪法和法律中有与之相抵触的内容。

上述参议员和众议员，各州州议会议员，以及合众国和各州所有行政和司法官员，应宣誓或作代誓宣言拥护本宪法；但决不得以宗教信仰作为担任合众国属下任何官职或公职的必要资格。

### 第七条

经九个州制宪会议的批准，即足以使本宪法在各批准州成立。

Done in Convention by the Unanimous Consent of the States present the Seventeenth Day of September in the Year of our Lord one thousand seven hundred and Eighty seven and of the Independance of the United States of America the Twelfth In witness whereof We have hereunto subscribed our Names.

G°. Washington

Presidt and deputy from Virginia

**Delaware**

Geo: Read                          Gunning Bedford jun

John Dickinson                  Richard Bassett

Jaco: Broom

**Maryland**

James McHenry                 Dan of St Thos. Jenifer

Danl. Carroll

**Virginia**

John Blair                            James Madison Jr.

**North Carolina**

Wm. Blount                        Richd. Dobbs Spaight

Hu Williamson

**South Carolina**

J. Rutledge                          Charles Cotesworth Pinckney

Charles Pinckney              Pierce Butler

**Georgia**

William Few                       Abr Baldwin

**New Hampshire**

John Langdon                     Nicholas Gilman

　　本宪法于耶稣纪元一千七百八十七年，即美利坚合众国独立后第十二年的九月十七日，经出席各州在制宪会议上一致同意后制定。我们谨在此签名作证。

**乔治·华盛顿**
**主席、弗吉尼亚州代表**
**特拉华州**

乔治·里德　　　　　　　　　　小冈宁·贝德福德

约翰·迪金森　　　　　　　　　理查德·巴西特

雅各布·布鲁姆

**马里兰州**

詹姆斯·麦克亨利　　　　　　　圣托马斯·詹尼弗的丹尼尔

丹尼尔·卡罗尔

**弗吉尼亚州**

约翰·布莱尔　　　　　　　　　小詹姆斯·麦迪逊

**北卡罗来纳州**

威廉·布朗特　　　　　　　　　理查德·多布斯·斯佩特

休·威廉森

**南卡罗来纳州**

约翰·拉特利奇　　　　　　　　查尔斯·科茨沃斯·平克尼

查尔斯·平克尼　　　　　　　　皮尔斯·巴特勒

**佐治亚州**

威廉·费尤　　　　　　　　　　亚伯拉罕·鲍德温

**新罕布什尔州**

约翰·兰登　　　　　　　　　　尼古拉斯·吉尔曼

**Massachusetts**

Nathaniel Gorham                    Rufus King

**Connecticut**

Wm. Saml. Johnson                  Roger Sherman

**New York**

Alexander Hamilton

**New Jersey**

Wil: Livingston                     David Brearley

Wm. Paterson                        Jona: Dayton

**Pennsylvania**

B Franklin                          Thomas Mifflin

Robt. Morris                        Geo. Clymer

Thos. FitzSimons                    Jared Ingersoll

James Wilson                        Gouv Morris

**Attest William Jackson Secretary**


**The Bill of Rights:**


**Amendment I**

Congress shall make no law respecting an establishment of religion, or prohibiting the free exercise thereof; or abridging the freedom of speech, or of the press; or the right of the people peaceably to assemble, and to petition the Government for a redress of grievances.

**马萨诸塞州**

 纳撒尼尔·戈勒姆 鲁弗斯·金

**康涅狄格州**

 威廉·塞缪尔·约翰逊 罗杰·谢尔曼

**纽约州**

 亚历山大·汉密尔顿

**新泽西州**

 威廉·利文斯顿 戴维·布里尔利

 威廉·帕特森 乔纳森·戴顿

**宾夕法尼亚州**

 本杰明·富兰克林 托马斯·米夫林

 罗伯特·莫里斯 乔治·克莱默

 托马斯·菲茨西蒙斯 贾雷德·英格索尔

 詹姆斯·威尔逊 古·莫里斯

 证人：威廉·杰克逊，秘书


**《权利法案》：**

（依照原宪法第五条、由国会提出并经各州批准、增添和修改美利坚合众国宪法的条款。译者注）

**第一条修正案**

〔前十条修正案于 1789 年 9 月 25 日提出，1791 年 12 月 15 日批准，被称为"权利法案"。〕

国会不得制定关于下列事项的法律：确立国教或禁止信教自由；剥夺言论自由或出版自由；或剥夺人民和平集会和向政府请愿伸冤的权利。

## Amendment II

A well regulated Militia, being necessary to the security of a free State, the right of the people to keep and bear Arms, shall not be infringed.

## Amendment III

No Soldier shall, in time of peace be quartered in any house, without the consent of the Owner, nor in time of war, but in a manner to be prescribed by law.

## Amendment IV

The right of the people to be secure in their persons, houses, papers, and effects, against unreasonable searches and seizures, shall not be violated, and no Warrants shall issue, but upon probable cause, supported by Oath or affirmation, and particularly describing the place to be searched, and the persons or things to be seized.

## Amendment V

No person shall be held to answer for a capital, or otherwise infamous crime, unless on a presentment or indictment of a Grand Jury, except in cases arising in the land or naval forces, or in the Militia, when in actual service in time of War or public danger; nor shall any person be subject for the same offence to be twice put in jeopardy of life or limb; nor shall be compelled in any criminal case to be a witness against himself, nor be deprived of life, liberty, or property, without due process of law; nor shall private property be taken for public use, without just compensation.

## Amendment VI

In all criminal prosecutions, the accused shall enjoy the right to a speedy and public trial, by an impartial jury of the State and district wherein the crime shall have been committed, which district shall have been previously ascertained by law, and to be informed of the nature and cause of the accusation; to be confronted with the witnesses against him; to have compulsory process for obtaining witnesses in his favor, and to have the Assistance of Counsel for his defence.

### 第二条修正案

管理良好的民兵是保障自由州的安全所必需的，因此人民持有和携带武器的权利不得侵犯。

### 第三条修正案

未经房主同意，士兵平时不得驻扎在任何住宅；除依法律规定的方式，战时也不得驻扎。

### 第四条修正案

人民的人身、住宅、文件和财产不受无理搜查和扣押的权利，不得侵犯。除依据可能成立的理由，以宣誓或代誓宣言保证，并详细说明搜查地点和扣押的人或物，不得发出搜查和扣押状。

### 第五条修正案

无论何人，除非根据大陪审团的报告或起诉书，不受死罪或其他重罪的审判，但发生在陆、海军中或发生在战时或出现公共危险时服役的民兵中的案件除外。任何人不得因同一犯罪行为而两次遭受生命或身体的危害；不得在任何刑事案件中被迫自证其罪；不经正当法律程序，不得被剥夺生命、自由或财产。不给予公平赔偿，私有财产不得充作公用。

### 第六条修正案

在一切刑事诉讼中，被告有权由犯罪行为发生地的州和地区的公正陪审团予以迅速和公开的审判，该地区应事先已由法律确定；得知控告的性质和理由；同原告证人对质；以强制程序取得对其有利的证人；取得律师帮助为其辩护。

### Amendment VII

In Suits at common law, where the value in controversy shall exceed twenty dollars, the right of trial by jury shall be preserved, and no fact tried by a jury, shall be otherwise re-examined in any Court of the United States, than according to the rules of the common law.

### Amendment VIII

Excessive bail shall not be required, nor excessive fines imposed, nor cruel and unusual punishments inflicted.

### Amendment IX

The enumeration in the Constitution, of certain rights, shall not be construed to deny or disparage others retained by the people.

### Amendment X

The powers not delegated to the United States by the Constitution, nor prohibited by it to the States, are reserved to the States respectively, or to the people.

The Constitution: Amendments 11-27

### AMENDMENT XI

Passed by Congress March 4, 1794. Ratified February 7, 1795.

Note: Article III, section 2, of the Constitution was modified by amendment 11.

The Judicial power of the United States shall not be construed to extend to any suit in law or equity, commenced or prosecuted against one of the United States by Citizens of another State, or by Citizens or Subjects of any Foreign State.

## 第七条修正案

在习惯法的诉讼中，其争执价额超过二十美元，由陪审团审判的权利应受到保护。由陪审团裁决的事实，合众国的任何法院除非按照习惯法规则，不得重新审查。

## 第八条修正案

不得要求过多的保释金，不得处以过重的罚金，不得施加残酷和非常的惩罚。

## 第九条修正案

本宪法对某些权利的列举，不得被解释为否定或轻视由人民保留的其他权利。

## 第十条修正案

宪法未授予合众国、也未禁止各州行使的权力，由各州各自保留，或由人民保留。

## 第十一条修正案

[1794 年 3 月 4 日提出，1795 年 2 月 7 日批准]

合众国的司法权，不得被解释为适用于由他州公民或任何外国公民或国民对合众国一州提出的或起诉的任何普通法或衡平法的诉讼。

## AMENDMENT XII

Passed by Congress December 9, 1803. Ratified June 15, 1804.

Note: A portion of Article II, section 1 of the Constitution was superseded by the 12th amendment.

The Electors shall meet in their respective states and vote by ballot for President and Vice-President, one of whom, at least, shall not be an inhabitant of the same state with themselves; they shall name in their ballots the person voted for as President, and in distinct ballots the person voted for as Vice-President, and they shall make distinct lists of all persons voted for as President, and of all persons voted for as Vice-President, and of the number of votes for each, which lists they shall sign and certify, and transmit sealed to the seat of the government of the United States, directed to the President of the Senate; -- the President of the Senate shall, in the presence of the Senate and House of Representatives, open all the certificates and the votes shall then be counted; -- The person having the greatest number of votes for President, shall be the President, if such number be a majority of the whole number of Electors appointed; and if no person have such majority, then from the persons having the highest numbers not exceeding three on the list of those voted for as President, the House of Representatives shall choose immediately, by ballot, the President. But in choosing the President, the votes shall be taken by states, the representation from each state having one vote; a quorum for this purpose shall consist of a member or members from two-thirds of the states, and a majority of all the states shall be necessary to a choice. [And if the House of Representatives shall not choose a President whenever the right of choice shall devolve upon them, before the fourth day of March next following, then the Vice-President shall act as President, as in case of the death or other constitutional disability of the President. --]* The person having the greatest number of votes as Vice-President, shall be the Vice-President, if such number be a majority of the whole number of Electors appointed, and if no person have a majority, then from the two highest numbers on the list, the Senate shall choose the Vice-President; a quorum for the purpose shall consist of two-thirds of the whole number of Senators, and a majority of the whole number shall be necessary to a choice. But no person constitutionally ineligible to the office of President shall be eligible to that of Vice-President of the United States.

### 第十二条修正案

［1803 年 12 月 9 日提出，1804 年 7 月 27 日批准 ］

选举人在各自州内集会，投票选举总统和副总统，其中至少有一人不是选举人本州的居民。选举人须在选票上写明被选为总统之人的姓名，并在另一选票上写明校选为副总统之人的姓名。选举人须将所有被选为总统之人和所有被选为副总统之人分别开列名单，写明每人所得票数；在该名单上签名作证，将封印后的名单送合众国政府所在地，交参议院议长收。参议院议长在参议院和众议院全体议员面前开拆所有证明书，然后计算票数。获得总统选票最多的人，如所得票数超过所选派选举人总数的半数，即为总统。如无人获得这种过半数票，众议院应立即从被选为总统之人名单中得票最多的但不超过三人中间，投票选举总统。但选举总统时，以州为单位计票，每州代表有一票表决权。三分之二的州各有一名或多名众议员出席，即构成选举总统的法定人数，选出总统需要所有州的过半数票。［ 当选举总统的权力转移到众议院时，如该院在次年三月四日前尚未选出总统，则由副总统代理总统，如同总统死亡或宪法规定的其他丧失任职能力的情况一样。］(11)得副总统选票最多的人，如所得票数超过所选派选举人总数的半数，即为副总统。如无人得过半数票，参议院应从名单上得票最多的两人中选举副总统。选举副总统的法定人数由参议员总数的三分之二构成，选出副总统需要参议员总数的过半数票。但依宪法无资格担任总统的人，也无资格担任合众国副总统。

*Superseded by section 3 of the 20th amendment.

## AMENDMENT XIII
Passed by Congress January 31, 1865. Ratified December 6, 1865.

Note: A portion of Article IV, section 2, of the Constitution was superseded by the 13th amendment.

**Section 1**    Neither slavery nor involuntary servitude, except as a punishment for crime whereof the party shall have been duly convicted, shall exist within the United States, or any place subject to their jurisdiction.

**Section 2**    Congress shall have power to enforce this article by appropriate legislation.

## AMENDMENT XIV
Passed by Congress June 13, 1866. Ratified July 9, 1868.

Note: Article I, section 2, of the Constitution was modified by section 2 of the 14th amendment.

**Section 1**    All persons born or naturalized in the United States, and subject to the jurisdiction thereof, are citizens of the United States and of the State wherein they reside. No State shall make or enforce any law which shall abridge the privileges or immunities of citizens of the United States; nor shall any State deprive any person of life, liberty, or property, without due process of law; nor deny to any person within its jurisdiction the equal protection of the laws.

**Section 2**    Representatives shall be apportioned among the several States according to their respective numbers, counting the whole number of persons in each State, excluding Indians not taxed. But when the right to vote at any election for the choice of electors for President and Vice-President of the United States, Representatives in Congress, the Executive and Judicial officers of a State, or the members of the Legislature thereof, is denied to any of the male inhabitants of such State, being twenty-one years of age,* and citizens of the United States, or in any way abridged, except for participation in rebellion, or other crime, the basis of representation therein shall be reduced in the proportion which the number of such male citizens shall bear to the whole number of male citizens twenty-one years of age in such State.

## 第十三条修正案

［1865 年 1 月 31 日提出，1865 年 12 月 6 日批准］

第一款　在合众国境内受合众国管辖的任何地方，奴隶制和强制劳役都不得存在，但作为对于依法判罪的人的犯罪的惩罚除

第二款　国会有权以适当立法实施本条。

## 第十四条修正案

［1866 年 6 月 13 日提出，1868 年 7 月 9 日批准］

第一款　所有在合众国出生或归化合众国并受其管辖的人，都是合众国的和他们居住州的公民。任何一州，都不得制定或实施限制合众国公民的特权或豁免权的任何法律；不经正当法律程序，不得剥夺任何人的生命、自由或财产；在州管辖范围内，也不得拒绝给予任何人以平等法律保护。

第二款　众议员名额，应按各州人口比例进行分配，此人口数包括一州的全部人口数，但不包括未被征税的印第安人。但在选举合众国总统和副总统选举人、国会众议员、州行政和司法官员或州议会议员的任何选举中，一州的［年满二十一岁］⑫并且是合众国公民的任何男性居民，除因参加叛乱或其他犯罪外，如其选举权道到拒绝或受到任何方式的限制，则该州代表权的基础，应按以上男性公民的人数同该州年满二十一岁男性公民总人数的比例予以削减。

**Section 3**    No person shall be a Senator or Representative in Congress, or elector of President and Vice-President, or hold any office, civil or military, under the United States, or under any State, who, having previously taken an oath, as a member of Congress, or as an officer of the United States, or as a member of any State legislature, or as an executive or judicial officer of any State, to support the Constitution of the United States, shall have engaged in insurrection or rebellion against the same, or given aid or comfort to the enemies thereof. But Congress may by a vote of two-thirds of each House, remove such disability.

**Section 4**    The validity of the public debt of the United States, authorized by law, including debts incurred for payment of pensions and bounties for services in suppressing insurrection or rebellion, shall not be questioned. But neither the United States nor any State shall assume or pay any debt or obligation incurred in aid of insurrection or rebellion against the United States, or any claim for the loss or emancipation of any slave; but all such debts, obligations and claims shall be held illegal and void.

**Section 5**    The Congress shall have the power to enforce, by appropriate legislation, the provisions of this article.

*Changed by section 1 of the 26th amendment.

### AMENDMENT XV

Passed by Congress February 26, 1869. Ratified February 3, 1870.

**Section 1**    The right of citizens of the United States to vote shall not be denied or abridged by the United States or by any State on account of race, color, or previous condition of servitude--

**Section 2**    The Congress shall have the power to enforce this article by appropriate legislation.

### AMENDMENT XVI

Passed by Congress July 2, 1909. Ratified February 3, 1913.

Note: Article I, section 9, of the Constitution was modified by amendment 16.

第三款　无论何人，凡先前曾以国会议员、或合众国官员、或任何州议会议员、或任何州行政或司法官员的身份宣誓维护合众国宪法，以后又对合众国作乱或反叛，或给予合众国敌人帮助或鼓励，都不得担任国会参议员或众议员、或总统和副总统选举人，或担任合众国或任何州属下的任何文职或军职官员。但国会得以两院各三分之二的票数取消此种限制。

第四款　对于法律批准的合众国公共债务，包括因支付平定作乱或反叛有功人员的年金和奖金而产生的债务，其效力不得有所怀疑。但无论合众国或任何一州，都不得承担或偿付因援助对合众国的作乱或反叛而产生的任何债务或义务，或因丧失或解放任何奴隶而提出的任何赔偿要求；所有这类债务、义务和要求，都应被认为是非法和无效的。

第五款　国会有权以适当立法实施本条规定。

## 第十五条修正案
［1869 年 2 月 26 日提出，1870 年 2 月 3 日批准］

第一款　合众国公民的选举权，不得因种族、肤色或以前是奴隶而被合众国或任何一州加以拒绝或限制。

第二款　国会有权以适当立法实施本条。

## 第十六条修正案
［1909 年 7 月 12 日提出，1913 年 2 月 3 日批准］

The Congress shall have power to lay and collect taxes on incomes, from whatever source derived, without apportionment among the several States, and without regard to any census or enumeration.

## AMENDMENT XVII

Passed by Congress May 13, 1912. Ratified April 8, 1913.

Note: Article I, section 3, of the Constitution was modified by the 17th amendment.

The Senate of the United States shall be composed of two Senators from each State, elected by the people thereof, for six years; and each Senator shall have one vote. The electors in each State shall have the qualifications requisite for electors of the most numerous branch of the State legislatures.

When vacancies happen in the representation of any State in the Senate, the executive authority of such State shall issue writs of election to fill such vacancies: Provided, That the legislature of any State may empower the executive thereof to make temporary appointments until the people fill the vacancies by election as the legislature may direct.

This amendment shall not be so construed as to affect the election or term of any Senator chosen before it becomes valid as part of the Constitution.

## AMENDMENT XVIII

Passed by Congress December 18, 1917. Ratified January 16, 1919. Repealed by amendment 21.

**Section 1**    After one year from the ratification of this article the manufacture, sale, or transportation of intoxicating liquors within, the importation thereof into, or the exportation thereof from the United States and all territory subject to the jurisdiction thereof for beverage purposes is hereby prohibited.

**Section 2**    The Congress and the several States shall have concurrent power to enforce this article by appropriate legislation.

**Section 3**    This article shall be inoperative unless it shall have been ratified as an amendment to the Constitution by the legislatures of the several States, as provided in the Constitution, within seven years from the date of the submission hereof to the States by the Congress.

国会有权对任何来源的收入规定和征收所得税，无须在各州按比例进行分配，也无须考虑任何人口普查或人口统计。

## 第十七条修正案

［1912 年 5 月 13 日提出，1913 年 4 月 8 日批准］

合众国参议院由每州人民选举的两名参议员组成，任期六年；每名参议员有一票表决权。每个州的选举人应具备该州州议会人数最多一院选举人所必需的资格。

任何一州在参议院的代表出现缺额时，该州行政当局应发布选举令，以填补此项缺额。但任何一州的议会，在人民依该议会指示举行选举填补缺额以前，得授权本州行政长官任命临时参议员。

本条修正案不得作如此解释，以致影响在本条修正案作为宪法的一部分生效以前当选的任何参议员的选举或任期。

## 第十八条修正案

［1917 年 12 月 18 日提出，1919 年 1 月 16 日批准］

［第一款　本条批准一年后，禁止在合众国及其管辖下的一切领土内酿造、出售和运送作为饮料的致醉酒类；禁止此类酒类输入或输出合众国及其管辖下的一切领土。

第二款　国会和各州都有权以适当立法实施本条。

第三款　本条除非在国会将其提交各州之日起七年以内，由各州议会按本宪法规定批准为宪法修正案，不得发生效力。］⑬

## AMENDMENT XIX

Passed by Congress June 4, 1919. Ratified August 18, 1920.

The right of citizens of the United States to vote shall not be denied or abridged by the United States or by any State on account of sex.

Congress shall have power to enforce this article by appropriate legislation.

## AMENDMENT XX

Passed by Congress March 2, 1932. Ratified January 23, 1933.

Note: Article I, section 4, of the Constitution was modified by section 2 of this amendment. In addition, a portion of the 12th amendment was superseded by section 3.

**Section 1**    The terms of the President and the Vice President shall end at noon on the 20th day of January, and the terms of Senators and Representatives at noon on the 3d day of January, of the years in which such terms would have ended if this article had not been ratified; and the terms of their successors shall then begin.

**Section 2**    The Congress shall assemble at least once in every year, and such meeting shall begin at noon on the 3d day of January, unless they shall by law appoint a different day.

**Section 3**    If, at the time fixed for the beginning of the term of the President, the President elect shall have died, the Vice President elect shall become President. If a President shall not have been chosen before the time fixed for the beginning of his term, or if the President elect shall have failed to qualify, then the Vice President elect shall act as President until a President shall have qualified; and the Congress may by law provide for the case wherein neither a President elect nor a Vice President shall have qualified, declaring who shall then act as President, or the manner in which one who is to act shall be selected, and such person shall act accordingly until a President or Vice President shall have qualified.

## 第十九条修正案

［1919 年 6 月 4 日提出，1920 年 8 月 18 日批准］

合众国公民的选举权，不得因性别而被合众国或任何一州加以拒绝或限制。

国会有权以适当立法实施本条。

## 第二十条修正案

［1933 年 3 月 2 日提出，1933 年 1 月 23 日批准］

第一款　总统和副总统的任期应在本条未获批准前原定任期届满之年的一月二十日正午结束，参议员和众议员的任期在本条未获批准前原定任期届满之年的一月三日正午结束，他们继任人的任期在同时开始。

第二款　国会每年至少应开会一次，除国会以法律另订日期外，此会议在一月三日正午开始。

第三款　如当选总统在规定总统任期开始的时间已经死亡，当选副总统应成为总统。如在规定总统任期开始的时间以前，总统尚未选出，或当选总统不合乎资格，则当选副总统应代理总统直到一名总统已合乎资格时为止。在当选总统和当选副总统都不合乎资格时，国会得以法律规定代理总统之人，或宣布选出代理总统的办法。此人应代理总统直到一名总统或副总统合乎资格时为止。

**Section 4**   The Congress may by law provide for the case of the death of any of the persons from whom the House of Representatives may choose a President whenever the right of choice shall have devolved upon them, and for the case of the death of any of the persons from whom the Senate may choose a Vice President whenever the right of choice shall have devolved upon them.

**Section 5**   Sections 1 and 2 shall take effect on the 15th day of October following the ratification of this article.

**Section 6**   This article shall be inoperative unless it shall have been ratified as an amendment to the Constitution by the legislatures of three-fourths of the several States within seven years from the date of its submission.

## AMENDMENT XXI

Passed by Congress February 20, 1933. Ratified December 5, 1933.

**Section 1**   The eighteenth article of amendment to the Constitution of the United States is hereby repealed.

**Section 2**   The transportation or importation into any State, Territory, or Possession of the United States for delivery or use therein of intoxicating liquors, in violation of the laws thereof, is hereby prohibited.

**Section 3**   This article shall be inoperative unless it shall have been ratified as an amendment to the Constitution by conventions in the several States, as provided in the Constitution, within seven years from the date of the submission hereof to the States by the Congress.

## AMENDMENT XXII

Passed by Congress March 21, 1947. Ratified February 27, 1951.

**Section 1**   No person shall be elected to the office of the President more than twice, and no person who has held the office of President, or acted as President, for more than two years of a term to which some other person was elected President shall be elected to the office of President more than once. But this Article shall not apply to any person holding the office of President when this Article was proposed by Congress, and shall not prevent any person who may be holding the office of President, or acting as President, during the term within which this Article becomes operative from holding the office of President or acting as President during the remainder of such term.

第四款　国会得以法律对以下情况作出规定：在选举总统的权利转移到众议院时，而可被该院选为总统的人中有人死亡；在选举副总统的权利转移到参议院时，而可被该院选为副总统的人中有人死亡。

第五款　第一款和第二款应在本条批准以后的十月十五日生效。

第六款　本条除非在其提交各州之日起七年以内，自四分之三州议会批准为宪法修正案，不得发生效力。

## 第二十一条修正案
［1933 年 2 月 20 日提出，1933 年 12 月 5 日批准］

第一款　美利坚合众国宪法修正案第十八条现予废除。

第二款　在合众国任何州、领地或属地内，凡违反当地法律为在当地发货或使用而运送或输入致醉酒类，均予以禁止。

第三款　本条除非在国会将其提交各州之日起七年以内，由各州制宪会议依本宪法规定批准为宪法修正案，不得发生效力。

## 第二十二条修正案
［1947 年 3 月 24 日提出，1951 年 2 月 27 日批准］

第一款　无论何人，当选担任总统职务不得超过两次；无论何人，在他人当选总统任期内担任总统职务或代理总统两年以上，不得当选担任总统职务一次以上。但本条不适用于在国会提出本条时正在担任总统职务的任何人；也不妨碍本条在一届总统任期内生效时正在担任总统职务或代理总统的任何人，在此届任期结束前继续担任总统职务或代理总统。

**Section 2**    This article shall be inoperative unless it shall have been ratified as an amendment to the Constitution by the legislatures of three-fourths of the several States within seven years from the date of its submission to the States by the Congress.

## AMENDMENT XXIII

Passed by Congress June 16, 1960. Ratified March 29, 1961.

**Section 1**    The District constituting the seat of Government of the United States shall appoint in such manner as Congress may direct:

A number of electors of President and Vice President equal to the whole number of Senators and Representatives in Congress to which the District would be entitled if it were a State, but in no event more than the least populous State; they shall be in addition to those appointed by the States, but they shall be considered, for the purposes of the election of President and Vice President, to be electors appointed by a State; and they shall meet in the District and perform such duties as provided by the twelfth article of amendment.

**Section 2**    The Congress shall have power to enforce this article by appropriate legislation.

## AMENDMENT XXIV

Passed by Congress August 27, 1962. Ratified January 23, 1964.

**Section 1**    The right of citizens of the United States to vote in any primary or other election for President or Vice President, for electors for President or Vice President, or for Senator or Representative in Congress, shall not be denied or abridged by the United States or any State by reason of failure to pay poll tax or other tax.

**Section 2**    The Congress shall have power to enforce this article by appropriate legislation.

## AMENDMENT XXV

Passed by Congress July 6, 1965. Ratified February 10, 1967.

Note: Article II, section 1, of the Constitution was affected by the 25th amendment.

第二款　本条除非在国会将其提交各州之日起七年以内，由四分之三州议会批准为宪法修正案，不得发生效力。

### 第二十三条修正案

［1960 年 6 月 16 日提出，1961 年 3 月 29 日批准］

第一款　合众国政府所在的特区，应依国会规定方式选派：一定数目的总统和副总统选举人，其人数如同特区是一个州一样，等于它在国会有权拥有的参议员和众议员人数的总和，但不得超过人口最少之州的选举人人数。他们是在各州所选派的举人以外增添的人，但为了选举总统和副总统的目的，应被视为一个州选派的选举人；他们在特区集会，履行第十二条修正案所规定的职责。

第二款　国会有权以适当立法实施本条。

### 第二十四条修正案

［1962 年 8 月 27 日提出，1964 年 1 月 23 日批准］

第一款　合众国公民在总统或副总统、总统或副总统选举人、或国会参议员或众议员的任何预选或其他选举中的选举权，不得因未交纳任何人头税或其他税而被合众国或任何一州加以拒绝或限制。

第二款　国会有权以适当立法实施本条。

### 第二十五条修正案

［1965 年 7 月 6 日提出，1967 年 2 月 10 日批准］

**Section 1**    In case of the removal of the President from office or of his death or resignation, the Vice President shall become President.

**Section 2**    Whenever there is a vacancy in the office of the Vice President, the President shall nominate a Vice President who shall take office upon confirmation by a majority vote of both Houses of Congress.

**Section 3**    Whenever the President transmits to the President pro tempore of the Senate and the Speaker of the House of Representatives his written declaration that he is unable to discharge the powers and duties of his office, and until he transmits to them a written declaration to the contrary, such powers and duties shall be discharged by the Vice President as Acting President.

**Section 4**    Whenever the Vice President and a majority of either the principal officers of the executive departments or of such other body as Congress may by law provide, transmit to the President pro tempore of the Senate and the Speaker of the House of Representatives their written declaration that the President is unable to discharge the powers and duties of his office, the Vice President shall immediately assume the powers and duties of the office as Acting President.

Thereafter, when the President transmits to the President pro tempore of the Senate and the Speaker of the House of Representatives his written declaration that no inability exists, he shall resume the powers and duties of his office unless the Vice President and a majority of either the principal officers of the executive department or of such other body as Congress may by law provide, transmit within four days to the President pro tempore of the Senate and the Speaker of the House of Representatives their written declaration that the President is unable to discharge the powers and duties of his office. Thereupon Congress shall decide the issue, assembling within forty-eight hours for that purpose if not in session. If the Congress, within twenty-one days after receipt of the latter written declaration, or, if Congress is not in session, within twenty-one days after Congress is required to assemble, determines by two-thirds vote of both Houses that the President is unable to discharge the powers and duties of his office, the Vice President shall continue to discharge the same as Acting President; otherwise, the President shall resume the powers and duties of his office.

第一款　如遇总统被免职、死亡或辞职，副总统应成为总统。

第二款　凡当副总统职位出缺时，总统应提名一名副总统，经国会两院都以过半数票批准后就职。

第三款　凡当总统向参议院临时议长和众议院议长提交书面声明，声称他不能够履行其职务的权力和责任，直至他向他们提交一份相反的声明为止，其权力和责任应由副总统作为代理总统履行。

第四款　凡当副总统和行政各部长官的多数或国会以法律设立的其他机构成员的多数，向参议院临时议长和众议院议长提交书面声明，声称总统不能够履行总统职务的权力和责任时，副总统应立即作为代理总统承担总统职务的权力和责任。

此后，当总统向参议院临时议长和众议院议长提交书面声明，声称丧失能力的情况不存在时，他应恢复总统职务的权力和责任，除非副总统和行政各部长官的多数或国会以法律设立的其它机构成员的多数在四天之内向参议院临时议长和众议院议长提交书面声明，声称总统不能够履行总统职务的权力和责任。在此种情况下，国会应决定这一问题，如在休会期间，应为此目的在四十八小时以内集会。如国会在收到后一书面声明后的二十一天以内，或如适逢休会期间，则在国会按照要求集会以后的二十一天以内，以两院的三分之二的票数决定总统不能够履行总统职务的权力和责任，副总统应继续作为代理总统履行总统职务的权力和责任；否则总统应恢复总统职务的权力和责任。

## AMENDMENT XXVI

Passed by Congress March 23, 1971. Ratified July 1, 1971.

Note: Amendment 14, section 2, of the Constitution was modified by section 1 of the 26th amendment.

**Section 1**    The right of citizens of the United States, who are eighteen years of age or older, to vote shall not be denied or abridged by the United States or by any State on account of age.

**Section 2**    The Congress shall have power to enforce this article by appropriate legislation.

## AMENDMENT XXVII

Originally proposed Sept. 25, 1789. Ratified May 7, 1992.

No law, varying the compensation for the services of the Senators and Representatives, shall take effect, until an election of representatives shall have intervened.

### 第二十六条修正案

[1971 年 3 月 23 日提出，1971 年 7 月 1 日批准]

第一款 年满十八岁和十八岁以上的合众国公民的选举权，不得因为年龄而被合众国或任何一州加以拒绝或限制。

第二款 国会有权以适当立法实施本条。

### 第二十七条修正案

[1989 年 9 月 25 日提出，1992 年 5 月 7 日批准]

改变参议员和众议员服务报酬的法律，在众议员选举举行之前不得生效。

（本译本引用自李道揆《美国政府和美国政治》，商务印书馆，1999-03 版）